IRELAND'S COUNTRYSIDE
by H. M. FitzPatrick

FRONT COVER — GLENCAR
Situated in the heart of the Kerry Mountains
on the road through Ballaghasheen Pass from
Waterville to Ki'lorglin, Glencar is an
ideal base for hill walking and climbing
and there is salmon fishing in the Caragh
River.

INSIDE FRONT COVER — ROUND TOWER
The Round Tower is distinctly Irish—there
are more than 100 here but only a few in
Scotland, presumably erected by migrant monks.
The oldest towers date from the ninth century
and are thought to have been originally
put up as belfries. This one, at Ardmore, Co.
Waterford, was one the last to be built,
probably about 1200, soon after the coming of
the Normans. During the time of the Danish
raids the Round Towers served as hiding places
for sacred vessels and refuges for the monks.

IRELAND'S COUNTRYSIDE

by H. M. FitzPatrick

on behalf of
"TREES FOR IRELAND"

published by
David P. Luke

cover design
Karl Uhlemann

printed by
Leinster Leader Ltd.

The Red Squirrel is a pretty sight as it scampers through the tree tops, stopping now and then to take a peep at whoever has disturbed it. The nest of a squirrel is called a drey in which the young remain with their parents until the spring after birth. Food consists of acorns, hazel nuts and conifer seeds which it extracts from the cones by gnawing off the scales.

Contents

You don't have to go to the countryside to see wildlife—at Booterstown, a few miles from the city and beside the busy Dublin to Dun Laoghaire highway this Mallard Duck hatched out a fine clutch and is leading them on a little tour through the traffic.

OVERLEAF (pages 8 and 9)
An endearing group of young swallows looking with eyes of wonderment on the great world as they take their first trip from home out along a roof beam.
The Swallow winters south of the Mediterranean and comes to us in April and usually manages to rear two broods before assembling in great flocks before departure in August and September. Food is of flies, gnats and small beetles which it picks up whilst flying.
Numbers of Swallows have greatly diminished in the last few years, possibly due to the use of DDT against insects.

Foreword

THIS book is an introduction to Ireland's countryside, its lakes and hills, farms and forests and what may be seen in them. The canvas is vast and it would take many volumes to cover the subject exhaustively but it is hoped that this book will arouse the interest of everyone visiting country places end encourage them to pursue further reading in specialised works.

The author is a member of "Trees for Ireland" who, as a farmer, a forester and a naturalist, knows this country well. Publication has been greatly helped by a gift of £200 from Bowaters Irish Wallboard Mills, Ltd. and of £100 by an anonymous donor.

We have to thank many people and organisations for the free use of the photographs which are an important part of the book; acknowledgement is given separately.

OWEN MULHOLLAND
President
"Trees for Ireland"

Ninth Floor,
Fitzwilton House,
Wilton Place,
Dublin 2.

The Grand Canal links Dublin on the east coast with the Atlantic Ocean at Shannon and the south coast where the "Three Sisters" reach the sea in Waterford Harbour. The southern branch leaves the main canal at Lowtown, Robertstown and goes to join the River Barrow Navigation at Athy. The hotel at Robertstown shown in the picture is 20 miles from the city terminus, Portobello, and was the first "port of call" for passengers in the old days. The canal is once more in use for holidaymakers and cruisers and barges may be hired at Lowtown and Robertstown.

Chapter I

WHO OWNS THE COUNTRY ?

Farms, Woods, Parks, Mountains, Lakes, Rivers,
Seashore, Ancient Ruins and Monuments,
Public Paths and Rights-of-way and
Trespass.

OF the 20 million acres of land in the whole of Ireland the great bulk belongs to the farmers. Farmland, that is enclosed land utilised for grazing and tillage, in the Republic amounts to about $11\frac{1}{2}$ million acres and in Northern Ireland to just over $2\frac{1}{2}$ million acres. In addition, farmers have grazing rights on much of the mountain area which covers about $5\frac{1}{2}$ million acres in the entire country.

Forests, mainly woods and plantations belonging to the State, account for nearly 700,000 acres which are being added to all the time in the whole country—over 500,000 acres being in the South. Towns and villages, roads and other public lands, rivers and lakes occupy the rest, a small fraction of the area of our island.

Up to a hundred years ago the country was in the possession of a comparatively small number of landlords, descendants of those who had been awarded estates of thousands of acres of land confiscated after the wars from the first coming of the Normans in 1169 to the Battle of the Boyne in 1690. Some of it was occupied by the owners and was used as parks surrounding their mansions or as large farms worked by hired staffs of stewards and labourers. Stone walls, built in many cases as famine relief in 1840s, today still mark much of this parkland, with the remains of the "great houses", massive farmyards and winding avenues still to be seen. Nearly all of the estates, however, were rented out as separate

11

farms held by tenants on short leases and at high rents and there was much distress at times when agricultural prices were low. Distress led to dissatisfaction which gave rise to militancy and in turn to repression until at last the Government took action to get the farmers a better deal. Now, following a century of work by the Land Commission, every farmer has a right to the land he works, paid for, or in the process of being paid for, by annuities spread over many years.

This history of agitation against injustice should always be remembered if farmers seem a little over-jealous of their rights when outsiders enter on their fields. This and, of course, the obvious danger of trampling on crops and permitting cattle and sheep to stray through gates thoughtlessly left ajar.

Some of the parks and "home farms" escaped division into small holdings by the Land Commission and are owned by large proprietors, either descendants of the landlords of past centuries or later purchasers. They, too, may not welcome trespassers for some of the same reasons as the smaller farmers and with the added one that these places are often game preserves where every outsider is regarded with mistrust as a potential poacher.

Unless he has friends amongst the landowning community the visitor to the countryside is, therefore, in a straitjacket, confined to the roads and the few small areas of public land. Even the enjoyment of the seashore may be restricted if, as is so often the case, the land between the road and the strand is privately owned.

Top left:
As far as the eye can see! A Co. Down farmer shows the countryside to a visitor while Shep takes a rest. The pattern of fields, some under corn, others under grass stretches to the foot of the Mountains of Mourne and is typical of much of Ireland.

Bottom left:
The thatched cottages of the West have caught the eye of many a painter and here, near Clifden, an artist is busy putting on canvas this view of bogland and purple mountain. The loosely built dry stone walls are characteristic of this region.

13

*The second half of the month of May is Apple Blossom Time
in Co. Armagh. The route through the country of orchards is
signposted from Armagh through Loughgall, Ardress, Kilmore
and Markethill and is well worth the journey especially when
the trees are in bloom.*

Top left:
*The Vee Road zig-zags up the Knockmealdown Mountains
from Clogheen in Co. Tipperary and gives views of fine
scenery along its route to Lismore in the neighbouring county
of Waterford. Black-faced Mountain Sheep are the only livestock to be seen on the poor Red Sandstone soil of the hill
tops. The lower levels on the Tipperary side have large
forestry plantations of pines belonging to the State Services.*

Bottom left:
*Looking like a six-legged black beetle, these Aran fishermen
on Inisheer carry their currach down to the sea. These frail
craft are built of tarred canvas stretched on a light lath frame
and closely resemble the pre-historic coracles. They are
buoyant and manoeuverable and ride the Atlantic waves with
ease, and besides fishing they are used for passengers and
farm animals and for the transport of turf from the Galway
mainland.*

15

This leaves to the seeker of wide open spaces the unfenced mountains and the State forests; the former as we have seen covering over 5 million acres and the latter between north and south about 700,000 acres.

In most parts of Ireland walkers may freely enter on mountain land. That is not to say that it is without owners or that uninvited guns and dogs are welcome. All our land has owners who use it for sheep and cattle grazing, for turf cutting or for rearing grouse or other game birds. Some is held in common by a number of farmers, usually those living in the neighbourhood, or it is still attached to a local estate. These people usually do not mind walkers crossing their stretches of heather, or picnic parties, but may be expected to draw the line at fire lighting, camping or caravanning or the loosing of uncontrolled dogs.

In recent years many of the State Forests are open for public enjoyment. These are the older plantations where the trees have outgrown the danger of fire and where inflammable undergrowth, grass, heather and furze, have been smothered by the developing trees. Plantations of this age, 18 years upwards, have reached the thinning stage, that is some of the trees must be cut to give growing

Top left:

In Fermanagh lies Lough Erne, the country of Ulster's Lakeland where one-third of the area of the county is water—water for fishing in, water for sailing or cruising on, water for painting or photographing or just contemplating in peace. The lakeside road goes around the shore for 40 miles and provides many views over 20 miles of water and some of the 200 islands.

This is ideal country for camping and caravanning—there is a centre provided at Castle Archdale, 9 miles from Enniskillen. There is a wild fowl refuge and bird reserve at Castlecaulwell and a world famous pottery in nearby Belleek.

Bottom left:

Beside Boyle in Co. Roscommon is Lough Key Forest Park in the grounds of an ancient Cistercian Monastery the ruins of which remain near the bridge below the town. There is a marina, a restaurant and tourist centre, a wild-life reserve with Fallow Deer. a bog garden, forest and nature trails and picnic sites. Boats from the River Shannon have access to the lake.

The shingle beach at Derrymore, Co. Kerry with the pebbles worn smooth and rounded by the action of the waves.
The beach and the salt marsh behind it provide feeding for sea birds as well as sparse grazing for sheep. Places like this are excellent for bird watching.

Top left:
An Irish farmer guards his flock against foxes or dogs. Foxes carry off lambs and dogs kill grown sheep or cause a stampede leading to serious injury.
A shepherd does not welcome trespassers who disturb his sheep by crossing their grazing ground, especially if accompanied by dogs.

Bottom left:
Be sure to close the gate! (If you must climb it, get over at the sturdier hinge end). A stretch of Co. Donegal with many hedges which provide nesting places for lots of birds as well as shelter against wind for farm animals and crops. In some districts the line of the hedge is the only place where hardwood trees survive. Modern farming leads to their replacement with wire fences which is a pity as there is a whole world of animals, plants and insects living in the quiet and secret places of the hedgerow.
There is a booklet in the "I Spy" series.

19

A new born calf is carried into a warm dry shed in the farm-yard. Calves are reared in the open if they are left with their mothers but if the cow is to be milked for human use the calf is fed indoors "on the bucket" with milk diluted with 25% water. Milk is given for a month or so after which time it is gradually reduced as the calf will be eating hay and meals. The calf in the picture, a Hereford by its colour, was worth £50 in 1972.

space to the remainder. These thinnings are saleable and to get them to market the Forest Services have built miles of gravel roads which wind through the woods, and walkers are expected to keep to these roads, or, at most, to wander off them only by the "inspection paths" laid down for the use of the foresters. Cars are permitted only on specified forest roads, usually ones leading to car parks or view points and they are nearly all in forests which have been developed for public use with marked "trails", picnic sites and water supplies, shelters and toilets.

Fires and any activity which damages the trees are naturally enough frowned on by the foresters as are unleashed dogs. The woods are the haunts of birds and beasts and this interesting wild-life will never be seen if there are barking dogs about, or any other disturbance.

A list of "open forests" can be got from the Department of Lands and brochures on "nature trails" are on sale in the local forest. In Northern Ireland particulars should be sought from the Ministry for Agriculture.

Paths over which pedestrians have rights-of-way provide short cuts to church, village, river or seashore. The first are commonly known as Mass Paths and strictly speaking are intended solely for Sunday use going to church but few owners are so stringent about their use. Other paths have become rights-of-way through long usage, use by the public "from time immemorial" as the saying has it, and are usually provided with stiles or "bow gates" to exclude cattle and sheep. Public paths also lead to ancient ruins and monuments which are maintained by the Office of Public Works. These include churches and monasteries dating from early Christian times and more recent buildings erected after the coming of the Normans. All told, there are 800 monuments in State care, 1,200 megalithic tombs, 30,000 earthworks, often called "ring forts", 100 high crosses, 120 round towers and 350 Ogham stones. The megalithic tombs are of great age, 3,000 B.C. is the accepted date of some, and the country contains hundreds of chambered tombs, passage grave cairns, dolmens and stone circles.

The reaction of landowners to trespassing varies. Some do not object to people crossing their land provided gates are reclosed, crops respected and livestock left in peace; others resent the entry of any strangers, and visitors are well advised to seek permission

21

Due south of Oughterard in Connemara in the heart of the mountains thousands of acres have been planted by the Forest and Wildlife Service during the last twenty years. The picture shows a forest road through an infant plantation in the Cloosh Valley, a lovely walk for anyone looking for a good long tramp across the hills. A devastating forest fire can easily start in a plantation of this age and smokers are urged to take special care in these places.

Top left:
Bringing milk to the roadside stand for collection by lorry or, maybe, going the whole way to the creamery. Not long ago this was a job for the horse or donkey, now it is another task for the family car.
Loading churns is a daily chore on many farms especially in the dairy counties of Munster and in districts which send milk to towns and cities.

Bottom left:
A mountain forest at Glenmalure, Co. Wicklow. The dark trees on the damp soil at the foot of the hill are Spruce, on the poorer soil of the ridge are Pines.
This State owned forest, and many hundreds of others, is intersected by pleasant gravel roads which are open to the public for walking and picnicking and in some cases, for pony trekking. Fire lighting is forbidden in all forests.

23

before venturing onto private territory. Owners are entitled to request trespassers to leave immediately and to use "reasonable force" if there is resistence.

The laws of this country uphold private property and this includes protecting the rights of owners of lakes and rivers. Usually these belong to the riparian owners, that is, the owners of the lands bordering on them. Through custom and tradition, however, the public have the right to boat on our large lakes and major rivers, but this does not include the right to cross private land to gain access to the water. Neither does it permit a boat to be beached on the bank of the lake or river unless this is public land. The limitations of access and use are not well defined and a Court would be slow to recognise the existence of such rights unless there has been a long established exercise by the public of such a right

The sea and the foreshore up to high water level, but not sand dunes, are public property. As in the case of rivers and lakes, this does not mean that the public has a right of way to the shore and they can be effectively cut off from it by private land between a public highway and the coast.

Power is given in the 1965 Land Act to the Land Commission to deal with rights of way to rivers, lakes and sea and also with ancillary rights to park vehicles and to moor, anchor and beach boats. This enactment applies in the Republic only.

Finally—

A FEW SIMPLE RULES

1. Don't enter on private land without permission.
2. Don't disturb livestock on farms.
3. Don't walk through meadows or corn fields—if you must cross them, keep to the margins.
4. If a gate is closed and fastened, make sure it is left that way.
5. Don't start fires.
6. Don't scatter litter. Sweet wrappings, cigarette cartons and all papers are unsightly; empty bottles may injure people or animals. All such things should be brought home.
7. Don't dig up wild plants; some are rare and may be exterminated if many are removed. Even common ones should be left for others to enjoy.

Chapter II

COUNTRY WORK

(1) *Seasonal work on farms; tillage operations, crops commonly cultivated and farm livestock.*

A lot of "spectator farming" may have to be exercised across the hedge from the road, but even so, a little knowledge of what goes on on the land can add immeasurably to the enjoyment of a day in the country. A farmer friend, and, in Ireland, few are without one or two, can multiply this enjoyment many times by inviting the visitor onto the land itself.

Tillage work on a farm is seasonal. Ploughing starts in October and continues right through the winter provided the soil is dry enough. Nowadays it is done with a tractor which pulls two or three ploughs able to go down seven or eight inches to turn over furrows right across a field. In front of each plough travels a disc coulter which cuts the edge of the sod, then follows a skim coulter which pares off a light ribbon of the surface grass or stubble and then the plough proper with its curved mouldboard undercutting, lifting and reversing the sod and laying it in the furrow left by the preceding plough. The purpose of ploughing is to bury straw, grass and weeds and to leave a clean surface of soil which the winter frost and rain will break down into a loose seed bed for next year's sowing. Usually the practice is to plough stubble, that is, fields which had a corn crop in the season just over, as soon as possible after the autumn harvest, followed by "broken ground" which had potatoes or another root crop provided it is fairly dry and finally, when the last bite has been grazed off it during the hungry months of winter, the grass fields or lea ground which will be sown with corn in the spring. Usually some of the corn of last

A peaceful scene which becomes rarer every year. A good ploughman with a pair of smart horses can turn over an acre of stubble land in a long day's work. The job well done leaves all the straw buried and the soil exposed to the rains and frosts of winter which will reduce it to a fine tilth for the spring sowing.

Right:

A ploughman "starting the sett" in a pasture field, "a lea sod", which he is ploughing in mid-winter for sowing in the spring with corn—oats, wheat or barley. The first runs across the field, "opening the middle", require great skill and perfect control over the horses if the furrows are to run true and straight from headland to headland.

26

year will have been "under-sown" with hay seed to give a meadow for one, two, or three years ahead and, in that case, the stubble is not ploughed—the only treatment is picking "field stones" which would injure the mowing machine, and a heavy rolling and, perhaps, a dressing with fertilisers, artificial "bag stuff" or farmyard manure spread on the surface.

The ordinary plough turns the sod in one direction only, to the right, which means that a field is ploughed in "sets", travelling to and fro on each side of a "middle". There may be one middle in a small field or a number on a large area in which case when finished there are a series of sections each with its middle of two sods turned towards each other and separated from the next section by a furrow resulting from two sods turned away from each other.

In the springtime comes the harrowing, the breaking of the sods to a depth of several inches to give a seed bed and "cover" for the corn. For cereals, that is wheat, barley and oats, it suffices to give two runs with a disc harrow which consists of a number of discs mounted on a frame which cut into the soil and reduce it to a fine

A six furrow tractor plough does the job at a stroke. The long straw left by a Combine Harvester is not easy to bury and this multiple plough is doing it well.

"tilth". After discing, the surface is levelled by a zig-zag harrow, a gate-like affair with short spikes in staggered rows.

Corn is sown as soon as the land is dry enough not to adhere to the wheels of tractors and sowing machines. It is put in with a "combine drill", a device which applies concentrated fertiliser beneath the seed corn so that it is immediately available to the growing plant. Then comes a final run with a light zig-zag harrow and, perhaps, a roller to consolidate the soil if it is loose. And that finishes the job for the time being.

For a root crop of potatoes, beet, mangolds or turnips, the soil needs deeper cultivation than is necessary for cereals. This is done by rigid or spring toothed "grubbers" or by a rotovator which breaks up the soil to a depth of nine inches or so. A second ploughing across the direction of the first may be done to get a good tilth. These crops in most cases are treated with farmyard manure, a mixture of straw-bedding and dung rotted down in a compost heap, and this dressing and artificial fertilisers can be spread in the course of the cultivations and covered by the second ploughing. At one time all root crops were sown on "drills", that is, mounds two feet or so wide formed by a "double mould board" or drilling plough, but now these are employed only for potatoes, all other roots being usually grown in rows on the level surface of the field.

Every farmer endeavours to get his crops sown as early as possible in spring. This work is affected by the weather, continued rain can delay tillage, by the amount of help and implements at his disposal and, of course, by the acreage to be covered. March and April are the busy months; April sees the finishing touches and May the after-sowing jobs, spraying against weeds, a final rolling of cereals and meadows and a general tidying-up before the rush of silage and hay-making.

The greatest advance in agriculture in the last hundred years was due to the invention of the mowing machine. In the old days meadows and corn had to be cut by hand, which meant employing men with scythes, a slow, laborious way of work although we hear of experts mowing one acre in a day. The horse-drawn mowing machine is based on the principle of the scissors and consists of a "knife" of sharp edged "sections" reciprocating in an arm with projecting comb-like points, "fingers", and operated by the

29

ground-wheels. This device, worked by one man and pulled by two horses, speeded up harvesting tremendously and is still used on up-to-date tractor driven machines.

Silage-making starts in May and the cutting of the meadow may be done with a mowing machine, followed by a "buck-rake" gathering up the grass whilst still green, or the whole job may be handled by a sophisticated "forage harvester" which cuts and loads into a trailer. In whatever way it is cut and transported, the grass is piled into a pit, clamp or silo where it is compressed into a solid mass and preserved by fermentation as a nutritious food for stock during the coming winter.

Hay is cut and saved in late June or early July when the grass and clover in the meadow has formed seed heads but before seed has developed. It is cut by the machine travelling around the field in ever narrowing circuits, laying the mown grass in an even

Left:
A many tined cultivator is drawn over the ploughed ground to break up the soil.

The tractor draws a potato planting machine in a dead straight line, opening and closing the drills as it goes.

This young farmer must keep his mind on the work of placing the seed potatoes one by one in the revolving wheel which drops them at correct spacings in the furrow. A second operator sits in the near seat.

"swathe". It will be let lie in the swathe for one or two days depending on the weather and then turned or shaken up by a "hay-kicker", "tedder" or "side-delivery rake". When it is dry and sweet-smelling it is fit for "cocking" or for "baling". Deciding on its fitness calls for great judgement: if done too soon the hay heats and becomes mouldy, if left too long it gets over-dry, loses much of its food-value and palatability or gets caught by rain. Cocking is a time-honoured operation and, if help is available, still the best and safest way of saving hay. The hay is "windrowed" in long ridges, then gathered to the site of the cocks where it is built up by hand with forks—two good workers can put up a cock in ten minutes. Later comes raking down, pulling out the loose hay at the base, "heading" and roping to prevent scattering in strong winds.

The sandy Castlegregory Promitory separates Brandon Bay from Tralee Bay on the north side of the Dingle Peninsula. The soil suits onion growing which is a local industry.
The picture shows a horse drawn hay rake used to gather the hay for building into cocks. To the left of the driver's seat is a lever for raising the curved teeth of the rake to release the gathered hay.

Baling is done direct from the windrows either by a square baler or a round baler. The former gathers the hay into a chamber where it is compressed by a ram, trimmed by side knives and tied with twine. The machine travels continuously, dropping the tied bales onto the ground or onto a platform which gathers them into groups for ease of stacking. Usually they are stacked in lots of six or seven and left for three weeks or a month to mature. The rotary baler also collects the hay from the windrow and wraps it into a compressed cylindrical bale, wound round with twine. With older models the machine must stand still between one bale and the next so it travels in a series of stops and starts. Round bales are left to mature as they lie.

After the hay-making, and its gathering into ricks or hay barns, comes the harvest, beginning in August with the barley and stretching into October, Deire Fomhair, with the late wheat. At one time a back-breaking job, cutting with sickles or scythes, sheaf-binding and stooking, it progressed through the mowing-machine to the reaper and binder to the modern "combine harvester" which cuts and threshes in one operation. There is no more bringing in the corn at "harvest home", building the great stacks in the haggard ready for the big event, the threshing with upwards of forty men to organise and feed for two or three days. Now the "combine" and two men do it all, quietly, efficiently and, it must be admitted, unromantically.

The ordinary farm in Ireland is a "mixed farm"—a bit of tillage with corn, potatoes, mangels and turnips, a cow or two,

Top left:
Two Wicklow farmers saving the hay. Building it into field cocks is still the safest plan in broken weather. It is cut by mowing machine in June or early July, left lying for a day or two in the "swathe", turned over until it is partly dry, gathered up by hay rake or hay sweep and cocked. There is no smell nicer than "new mown hay"!

Bottom left:
A baler picks up the hay, packs it into rectangular bales and ties them with string or wire. The bales are stacked in groups of 6 or 8 and left for a few weeks to season before removal to a hay shed. This method is speedy and labour saving but bales are not weather proof and can take the rain and absorb ground damp. Round bales can be made with a special machine and are water proof.

some yearling cattle and, perhaps, a bunch of two-year-old "store cattle", a sow and a few fattening pigs. Nearly half, 40%, of our land is in small farms of below 50 acres which are run by family labour, and diversification rather than specialisation has been the tradition. Self-sufficiency is the aim. These small farms are mostly in Connacht and Counties Donegal, Longford and Cavan where indeed many of the holdings are below 30 acres. Medium sized farms, 50 acres and more, predominate in Munster and in Counties Wexford, Carlow, Kilkenny and Laois and the largest, in the 100 acre bracket, are to be found in the remaining seven counties of Leinster.

As might be expected, the pattern of farming changes between the small holdings of the west and the large ones of the eastern parts of the country. The small man is a rearer of stock, the large ranch owner a "finisher" of beef cattle. In between are the store cattle men and, by and large the tillage men too. The "typical" Irish farm is probably to be found in the 50-100 acre farms of Cork, Wexford, Kilkenny, Clare and Carlow, and they are certainly the most interesting for a visit. Here we can expect to find the full range of farm operations—a fair acreage of diverse tillage crops, up-to-date machinery and all the popular breeds of cattle and sheep.

The common Irish breed of cattle at one time was the Kerry—small, black, hardy, agile, easily fed and a fair yielder of milk and beef from sparse grazing land. In the last century the Short-

Top left:
Feeding hay to a trio of Hereford/Shorthorn store cattle which are spending the winter out of doors. All that is needed is to cut the twine from the bales, scatter the "plates" of compressed hay and let the animals tease it out themselves.

Bottom left:
The Kerries are descended from Celtic Black Cattle and were the principal breed in Ireland up to 1700 and are still important in Co. Kerry where a pure bred herd is kept in Killarney and an area from there to Dingle Bay is designated a "Kerry Cattle Area" where only bulls of the breed may be kept.
Kerries are primarily a dairy breed suited to rugged mountains where grazing is coarse and scarce. They are black, agile animals and very hardy.

Cattle feeding on a clamp of silage made from grass cut early in the summer and preserved by pressing tightly together and covering with polythene sheeting.
Pollution conscious farmers make sure that the liquid oozing from the clamp does not get into streams to kill fish.

horn was brought in from England and swept the board. To this day every non-pedigree beast in the country has a fair dash of Shorthorn blood. They are medium sized, red, with short incurved horns when these are permitted to grow. Those who favour the breed claim that it is "dual purpose", that is, the animals are good producers of milk and beef. The Department of Agriculture promoted them as "foundation stock" and encouraged farmers to keep Shorthorn cows for the dairy and to cross a proportion with bulls of purely beef breeds in order to produce store cattle for the fatteners. As time went on the "dual purpose" pure-bred Shorthorn divided into two sub-breeds, the Dairy Shorthorn, usually a red and white or red roan colour and a Beef Shorthorn, a heavier animal, usually dark red.

Two other long established breeds are the Hereford and the Aberdeen Angus, both beef breeds. The former is characterised by a white coloured head, farmers refer to them as "Whiteheads",

38

and a stocky body with red the predominant colour. The white head is a "dominant character" and calves have this mark if either parent has a strain of Hereford. Cross bred animals with white heads are highly regarded by feeders of beef cattle. The Aberdeen Angus is a small compact blocky animal, all black and hornless and known in the country as "black pollies", i.e. polled or hornless, a character which is dominant, like the white head in the Herefords. These are easily fed, hardy animals but they have lost favour on account of their small size. A breed which has forged ahead in recent years is the Friesian, a large-framed black

Some of a lot of 150 heifers shortly after arrival at Moyglare on the Kildare-Meath border near Maynooth. They will soon put on weight on this lush pasture. They are cross-bred store cattle with signs of Hereford, Shorthorn and, perhaps, Friesian strains.

These are "Store Cattle" and in 1971 over half a million were exported for a return of £55 million, that is an average price of £110 a beast.

The large black and white Friesian cows are great yielders of milk; good, well-fed ones give 2,000 gallons in a year, and are fine beef animals. The breed has become plentiful in recent years especially in Munster.

Top left:
Champion Aberdeen Angus cattle at the Dublin Spring Show. Known as "Black Pollies" because they are naturally polled or hornless, these cattle are raised for beef and are common in parts of the West and North-west but are losing popularity on account of their small size.

Bottom left:
Up near the Hell Fire Club in the Dublin Mountains life can be tough. The only bite of grass is near the shelter trees where the snow has been held back by the branches of the beech. These cross-bred Hereford cattle are hardy and will survive the snow if given a few forkfulls of hay each day.

41

The Ayrshire is a fine dairy breed from Scotland, more popular in Northern Ireland than in the Republic, and its high quality milk suits the liquid milk trade for domestic use. It is a hardy, easily maintained agile animal of compact build.

Right:
A bunch of Friesian Bulls. They are kept as sires in pure herds and for crossing with Shorthorn, Hereford and other breeds to improve size and milking qualities of offspring. They produce fast growing beef animals which reach impressive sizes.

and white animal which makes an excellent dairy cow, yields of 1,000 gallons a year are normal, and produces heavy, fast growing progeny for the beef trade. Farmers regarded Friesians as a profitable breed on better land and in consequence these piebald cattle are numerous in most parts of the lowlands. A rare, purely dairy breed is the Jersey, small, light weight, cream or chocolate coloured animals noted for the richness of their milk. They are of no value for beef and the bull calves are not reared unless intended for breeding purposes.

Tipperary, Cork, Kilkenny and Limerick are the great dairying counties where an important part of a farmer's income is from milk supplied to the butter and cheese-making creameries and to milk powder and chocolate crumb factories, but this type of farming is found to a less extent in other counties too, notably Kerry, Monaghan and Mayo. It tends to be a family business in the medium sized farms and the milking is nowadays more and more done by machines. The liquid milk trade is, naturally enough, concentrated in the neighbourhood of the cities and large towns: the Dublin supply is drawn from Kildare, Carlow, Meath, Wicklow and Co. Dublin itself whence it is collected daily by the retail firms.

From left to right—a white Shorthorn, a Black and White Friesian, a bunch of Jerseys and a second White Shorthorn. The Shorthorn and the Friesian are "dual purpose" breeds, profitable for the dairy and for beef. The Jersey is solely a dairy cow, a native of Jersey in the Channel Island group in the English Channel and yields rich cream milk sold at a premium.

Most dairy farmers sell off the calves when quite young as "suck calves" which are then reared to 15 or 18 months by small farmers. These are sold as "yearlings" to men with more extensive acreages and perhaps sold once more as "stores" to still larger farmers on the rich plain lands of Tipperary, Westmeath, Kildare and Meath. This procedure applies more specifically to bull calves: heifers may be reared by the dairyman as replacements for his milking herd or fattened for local sale.

Sheep breeds, unlike cattle breeds with the exception of the Kerry, are associated with definite territories in Ireland. Wicklow, Galway and Roscommon have their local breeds which are rarely seen outside these counties. The mountain districts of the south and west favour a black faced horned sheep and introduced breeds such as Border-Leicester and Suffolk are common on the

The Wicklow Cheviot Sheep are descended from a native breed of fine woolled mountain sheep which were crossed by Cheviot rams imported about 1850 by Kemmis of Ballinacor and Barton of Annamoe. They are small, all-white sheep, very active and hardy and with the ability to maintain themselves on sparse mountain grazing through the winter.

better land. The different breeds are easily distinguished: the Wicklow is all-white with no wool on its face, the Galway is also all-white too but has a tuft of wool on its forehead, the Mountain sheep are horned with black faces and long hair-like fleece, the Suffolk has a black face, no horns and tight curly wool. The Border Leicester is like the Wicklow but is larger and has a pronounced curved nose. Roscommon sheep are natives of the plains of that county and are rarely seen elsewhere. They are all-white, large, long-legged animals without the nimbleness associated with the Wicklow, Galway or Border Leicester breeds.

Shearing is done in the month of May when the weather has got warmer. Later comes dipping when the sheep are immersed in a bath of disinfectant to kill the mites which cause scab and other skin parasites.

The Oxford Down is a big sheep with a heavy coat of off-white wool, a brown face and a tuft of wool on its forehead. The rams are crossed with other breeds to produce fat lambs.

Top left:
A flock of "Wicklow Cheviots" passing through Laragh. Sheep are shorn of their wool in early summer and dipped in insecticide solution to rid them of pests. In the background is an attractive group of County Council houses.

Bottom left:
Black-faced horny sheep are on all our mountains outside the Wicklow Hills. They can subsist on the poorest land, nibbling grass and heather from amongst the rocks and rearing their lambs on bogs and hillsides of the south and west. They are less given to keeping in flocks than other breeds and will be seen scattered in twos and threes over the grazing ground. The wool is coarse in quality and is used mainly for carpet making.

Strange dogs are not welcome on a sheep farm! Even the most harmless one may cause sheep to stampede and do themselves severe injury.

Anyone travelling in Galway and adjacent districts will notice the hay ricks built around a mast or pole. This hay is for the winter feeding of sheep and cattle which help themselves direct

47

A mare and her two foals, an unusual sight as twins are extremely rare in horses. They will be left with their mother for four or five months and gradually weaned from a diet of milk onto solid food, bruised oats and hay. They are taught to lead with a halter and to get used to a bit, bridle and saddle until they are "made" ponies, two and a half to three years old, docile and obedient and fit for riding.

Right:
Sows and Bonhams on free range. They are Irish Large White breed, one of the two breeds permitted in the country, the other is the Landrace. All told there are about 3 million pigs in Ireland, reared and fattened for pork and bacon.

from the rick and the purpose of the pole is to prevent the rick over-turning when it is undermined.

In the days when every farmer with a fair sized farm kept two or three horses for ploughing and carting it was the practice to rear a few foals. The working mares were the "Irish Draught" type, strongly built lively animals with short hair on their feet, usually red or "bay" in colour with maybe one, two or three white hocks and with white "stars" on their foreheads. These were crossed with thoroughbred horses to produce hunters which would fetch good prices or "troopers" for army cavalry use which would be worth somewhat less. Now with tractors on the land horses are not much seen on farms and breeding is confined to specialists, stud farms and the "travelling people" who rear many a pony for the riding establishments. In any event, the pure Irish Draught mare in time became a rarity due to the pattern of breeding followed by the farmers, and the half-bred, three-quarter bred and nearly pure-bred mares which succeeded her did not possess the hardiness and agility of the Irish Draught.

Most small farmers keep a few pigs to consume surplus potatoes and skim milk supplemented by special "meals", or they go in

49

The Ass, or Donkey as it is usually called in Ireland, is the poor man's horse in many lands and is common in most parts of this country, especially in the West where it is used for carting and for carrying turf in panniers strung across its back. The Irish Donkey Society, 37 Cecil Street, Limerick, is working to improve the breed.

for a sow or two and sell the bonhams as soon as weaned. Specialists pig farmers who rear and fatten hundreds of pigs are becoming common. Until recently the only breed seen was the Large White but in the last few years, after much controversy, the Landrace, a North-European breed, longer bodied and leaner, was introduced and is now fairly common.

The "Monthly Fair", which for hundreds of years was the place where livestock of all kinds was sold, is slowly giving way to the "Auction Mart", usually a weekly event in a central point in a district formerly served by several fairs.

The old fashioned fair day was a colourful occasion with cattle, sheep, horses and their attendant drovers jam-packed in narrow streets where farmers sold to dealers in the midst of great noise and confusion. It was a difficult way of doing business and the "making of the bargain" called for a lot of astuteness and mind reading on the part of buyer and seller. Friends on both sides intervened in an endeavour to bring the deal to a conclusion with suggestions about "splitting the difference" and accusations that the stubborn one was a "hard man". After a sale all parties involved usually retired to a nearby public house to "wet the bargain". Later would come the payment with renewed wrangling about "luck money", an ill-defined discount allowed by the seller.

The Auction Marts have removed the cattle from the streets. Nowadays sales are conducted in paved yards with individual pens and a central auction ring where owners and buyers sit in tiers. Cattle are brought into the ring in lots and are sold to the highest bidder by public auction—the buyer and the seller paying

On the march! A flock of Geese in Co. Mayo step out for a day's grazing on the hills.
The domestic goose is thought to be descended from the Grey Lag breed from the far north which migrate southwards in Autumn.

a percentage commission to the company or co-operative running the mart. Sheep are usually sold in the pens, the auctioneer going from pen to pen with the buyers.

Country merchants and co-operatives handle most of the wheat grown on the farms, acting as agents for the millers, and paying according to a rate fixed by Government. The brewers and distillers buy their needs of barley direct from the growers at a price fixed by negotiation earlier in the year. Few farmers are in a position to store grain over the winter and the usual practice is to dispose of the lot as soon as possible after harvest, except a small portion held back for feeding to livestock or as seed for the next season.

Food Production is Ireland's greatest industry. In recent years in the entire country farm output totalled £365 million for livestock and livestock products and £70 million for crops of all kinds. This was the value of raw material; processed food comes to much more. From the Republic manufactured food and drink exported after meeting home needs brought in £180 million. If the value of live animals which were exported is added the amount is £252 million, more than one-half of our total exports of all kinds.

Top left:
In the West it is customary to let cattle and sheep feed directly from a circular hay stack, "a pike of hay", over the winter. When "self service" is practised it is usual to build the stack around a central pole which stops it toppling over as the animals undermine it.

Bottom left:
Up on the Wicklow Mountains by the Military Road turf is still cut by hand, pitching it from the bank by slane, a special spade with a wing so that two sides of the sod is severed in one stroke, spread and "footed" on the spreading ground until it is nearly dry, stacked in small heaps and finally transported to the hard road for the lorry. Bord na Mona do the job in style with giant machines which cut, spread, turn and transport the turf to electric power stations and to depots for domestic consumers. There are three sod powered electric generating stations and five stations which use milled peat i.e. broken into small pieces, operated by the E.S.B.

(2) *Seasonal work in Forests; raising trees from seed in nurseries, planting out in the woods, thinning plantations and felling timber trees.*

Nearly all afforestation in Ireland is done by the two State Services which over the past half century have built up a National Forest of close on 700,000 acres by 1972. They continue year by year to add to this area by further purchases of land too poor for agriculture, and its planting with trees.

Our Irish forests are nearly all conifers—that is pines, firs, spruces, larches and suchlike species. Oak, ash, beech and elm are planted only in small numbers. This is due to two reasons— first the soil of most of the land purchased is not fertile enough for the latter species, "hardwoods" as they are called, to grow into commercial timber and second the wood of conifers is far and away the sort most in demand—some 90% of our needs of timber are for "deal", that is mainly spruce and pine, and this market controls what is grown. Deal timber is used for joinery and house building, for box making, railway sleepers and all sorts of fencing as well as for pulping for paper making, wallboard and chipboard making. A further reason for concentrating on conifers is that these species grow at a very rapid rate, much faster than the hardwoods, they yield a good return of useful timber at an early age and in every way are a far more economic forestry proposition than any of the hardwood species.

Many people do not like conifers. They refer to them as alien and sigh for the "beautiful old-fashioned trees" of long ago. Most conifers are evergreen, which should be a mark in their favour, but is often held against them inasmuch as their critics say they always look the same and do not show the seasons of the year. This is not altogether true as even the most sombre pine or spruce puts out new shoots of verdant green each year which alters its look. In any case the comparison of a youthful conifer with an aged oak or other hardwood is not valid—trees acquire beauty and individual character with years and a young oak may be just as dull as a conifer and remain dull looking for much longer. Solid masses of conifers in their early days admittedly lack variety, especially if for reasons of soil and situation they consist of one species alone and the incorporation of a few brighter trees

*There are about 900 acres of tree nurseries run by the Forest
Services in the Republic and Northern Ireland which turn
out over 50 million 3 and 4 year old trees annually. The seed
is sown in long narrow beds and after one or two years in the
seed beds the seedlings are transplanted into lines and there
remain until large enough for final planting. The picture
shows in the foreground 2 year old Sitka Spruce seedlings, in
the middle one year beds protected against frost by branches
supported on wires and in the background transplant lines.
The man with the knapsac is spraying weed killer on the
alleys between the beds, the other men are hand weeding.*

such as larch and birch adds immensely to the charm of a block
of Scots pine or Sitka spruce.

The species which predominate in our forests are nearly all
foreigners. This is unavoidable as our native tree flora is small
indeed and contains only three species of commercial significance,
Oak, Ash and Pine. Altogether there are a bare dozen species—
Oak, Ash, Elm, Birch, Mountain Ash, Whitebeam, Cherry, Aspen,
Alder, Willow, Pine and Yew. Other woody plants found naturally

55

*Lifting 2 year old Sitka Spruce seedlings for transplanting.
They are prised up with forks and then pulled up carefully
in bunches in order to cause least damage to the fine feeding
roots.*

in Ireland are of small size such as Hazel, Hawthorn, Blackthorn,
Juniper, Furze, Apple, Arbutus, Broom and Holly. Our ancient
woods were nearly all Oak, the Sessile variety rare on the poorer
soils of the hills and the Pedunculate common in the more fertile
lowlands. On fresh soils, more especially where there was lime,
Ash grew either in admixture with Oak or by itself along the banks
of streams. Birch was found, as it is today, in clumps on hillsides
and the edges of bogs and creeping in as a "pioneer" species
where it found an opening in the forests of oak. Alder, Aspen
and Willow occupied land too damp for other species. The Pine
appears to have disappeared before historic times and our present
day "Scots" Pine is the same species re-introduced from Scotland
200 years or so ago.

By the end of the Middle Ages the Irish forests were reduced to a mere fragment of their former area, due to clearing for agriculture, felling to provide wood fuel for iron smelting or cutting down to remove cover from the Tories and Rapparees who raided the English settlements. By 1700 our native woods had almost entirely disappeared and the country was a "bleak, dreary waste for want of trees" according to a traveller who visited it in 1776. But replanting had already started and was to continue for another hundred years. It was done by the large landowners, the landlords as they were called, descendants of those settlers who had obtained grants of land from the Normans, the Tudors, the Stuarts, the Cromwellians up to the final confiscations and settlements after the Williamite war.

All our old trees are the result of this wave of planting. Avenues, ornamental clumps, shelter belts, park and hedgerow trees appeared in the demesnes. Some were of native species but

Is it worth keeping? The forester critically examines a young transplant of Sitka Spruce. In the middle is a man spraying weed killer, above is a tractor operated rotavator and men putting out seedlings into transplant lines.

gradually more and more foreign trees were brought in—Beech, Lime, Sycamore, Spanish and Horse Chestnut as well as many European conifers, Norway Spruce, Silver Fir, Larch and, of course, Scots Pine. Later came trees from further afield, Lebanon, Moroccan and Himalayan Cedars, Pines and Firs from Eastern North America and finally the splendid Western American species which today dominate our forests. Two of them, Sitka Spruce and Contorta Pine, both natives of the Pacific Coast regions of the United States and Canada, account for the bulk of our plantations, the former covers 55% of the State woods in Northern Ireland and 45% in the Republic and the latter 10% in the North and 30% in the South. Both are trees for bleak situations and wet acid soils, they are fast growers and produce large volumes of useful timber, especially the Sitka Spruce the wood of which is in strong demand for many purposes. Douglas Fir comes from the same region and has proved a valuable species in our Irish woods. The Larches also are common trees—the Japanese has reddish orange twigs and the European yellow twigs; both are deciduous and this habit helps them to give variety to blocks of evergreen conifers.

There are about 1,000 acres of nurseries in the country devoted to raising trees and the bulk of this area belongs to the State Services which turn out 50 million trees fit for planting each year, privately owned nurseries selling up to 4 million, in all sufficient for 30,000 acres of woods.

Seed sowing starts in April if the soil is dry enough and finishes in May. The usual practice is to sow broadcast in strips $3\frac{1}{2}$ feet wide after the soil has been worked into a fine tilth. This can be done by hand with spade, fork and rake but it is most often carried out by tractor operated implements, rotovator, bed shaper, and roller. The scattering of the seed is mechanised too, as is its covering with a $\frac{1}{4}$ to $\frac{1}{2}$ inch coating of fine gritty sand.

Weed seeds germinate before the harder coated tree seeds and this enables them to be dealt with by a light spraying with a weed killer—"a pre-emergence spray"—which saves much early hand work, but later weeds must be pulled out with care from amongst the tree seedlings.

In a year's time, or in two years depending on species, the young trees will be transplanted into rows, "lines" the forester

An expanse of Sitka Spruce 4 years after planting in Drum-keeran Forest, Co. Leitrim. Nearly half our forests are of this one species, a Pacific Coast tree which thrives on wet soil and produces a large volume of useful timber.

calls them, to allow more growing space and to develop a fibrous root system before the final shift to the regions of the open hillside or other rough ground where the new plantation is to be formed. This last step before setting in their permanent home may be for one or two years' duration, according to the species and the size of transplant required, so that plants leaving the nursery may be two years, three years or four years of age.

As much seed as possible is collected from good quality trees in Ireland but most is still imported from the countries where the trees are native. Oak acorns, Beech mast and Ash keys are gathered in autumn, the two former from the ground under the trees and the Ash from the branches, and there is usually enough for our needs, although in recent years a superior race of Beech has been brought in from Rumania. Minor species like Birch and Alder are also obtained at home. Their little "cones" are spread on sheets of paper and kept over the winter and in the springtime the seed readily sheds. The cones of Pine, Spruce and Larch are gathered direct off the trees in October and November and stored until March when the application of slight heat will cause the scales of the Pine and Spruce cones to open and release the seed. The Larch requires a vigorous threshing to break up the cones and free the seed. Silver Fir cones present no difficulty as they readily fall apart if stored in a dry place. The seed is separated from broken scales and wings by "winnowing" and by a little hand picking of foreign matter and it is then ready for sowing.

Visitors to State nurseries will be interested in the codes on the notice boards marking each lot of plants. These show the origin of the seed, the merchant who supplied it, the year of sowing and, with transplants, how long ago they were lifted from the beds and put out in the lines.

Trees are fit for planting in their final homes when still quite small. It is usual to put out Contorta Pine when no more than 6 inches high, Scots Pine at about 9 inches, Larch at a few inches more and the Spruces at 15 to 18 inches. These small sizes are the most economical in nursery time, transport and planting, but may result in greater cost for removing smothering weed growth on the planting ground over several years until the young tree overgrows it. The actual operation of planting is simplicity itself: a hole is dug with a spade, the plant is held in position at the

"Grand Fir", a fast growing American species, in compartment 39 Camolin Park State Forest, Co. Wexford. The age of conifers can be told from the whorls of branches which grow on the stem each year. In these trees the lower branches have been pruned off to produce clean knot-free timber but the stubs are still visible.

right depth, the soil is filled in on the roots and well firmed. Distance apart is 5 or 6 feet depending on species and it is usual to plant in straight lines the better to regulate the numbers of trees and to facilitate clearing of vegetation in the early years and the thinning of the plantation later on.

On wet or exceedingly poor soils the practice is to plough the land at 5 or 6 feet intervals with immense ploughs, pulled by crawler tractors, which turn up a big sod on top of which the young trees are planted. This gives them a great advantage over trees planted on the untouched surface of bog or heather mountain and a further boost to growth is achieved by applying about 2 ounces of fertiliser, usually Phosphate, to each plant.

After the trees are properly established with any failures replaced and their heads well clear of surrounding vegetation the plantation is left to its own devices for many years, never less than 15 and perhaps up to 20 years. All that is needed during this time is to keep the open drains free from blockages and to guard against fire. This last is the greatest danger to a plantation during its early growth before the branches have covered and killed inflammable ground vegetation and it is at its worst in late spring and early summer when grass and heather is tinder dry. Measures to combat fire taken by the Forest Services include notices warning the public of the danger from picnic fires and carelessly thrown matches, cigarettes and glowing pipes thoughtlessly knocked out, the appointment of local caretakers and patrolling by workers at week-ends and on holidays, "fire lines" between plantations and mountains from which heather fires might spread and look-out towers so that fires may be quickly spotted before they get serious. These towers are connected by telephone to the forester's house, and when he gets a report he calls out the forest "fire brigade" with fire and stirrup pumps, knapsack sprayers, shovels and beaters. In areas where fires are liable it is usual to form little reservoirs by damming mountain streams at easily accessible points.

In the young plantation the trees stand at 5 or 6 feet apart and their side branches soon "join hands" to cover the ground and encourage straight, clean stems to develop. When the lowest branches have died to a height of 6 feet as a result of congestion it will be time to consider a first thinning. This is the beginning of the forester's harvest. He thins the overcrowded "stand" of trees from about the fifteenth year onwards, removing some trees to give room to others, until by the fortieth year there remain only 150 or so of the original 1,200 or 1,700. In some cases these 150 "final crop" trees are ear-marked twenty years earlier and progressively "high pruned" of branches so that they will produce knot-free timber of good quality.

The early thinnings are light poles fit only for the mills which manufacture paper pulp, hardboard or chipboard. Later some will yield small logs suitable for sawing into narrow boards and at 30 years of age most will give a high proportion of "commercial" timber large enough for boards and scantlings. A profitable use for good straight trees of Douglas Fir, Scots Pine and Larch is found in supplying the needs of the Post Office and Electricity Supply Board for transmission poles. These are trimmed and peeled in the woods before transport to a creosoting plant for treatment against rot and insect damage.

Some of the thousand tons of conifer thinnings from young forestry plantations used weekly to manufacture Wallboard at Bowater's Athy factory, Co. Kildare.

Chipboard industries in Waterford, Scarriff, and Coleraine and Clondalkin Paper Mills consume similar large amounts of this material.

Work in the woods, more especially the carriage of timber, requires means of access, and all the State plantations are furnished with a close network of solid, gravel covered "extraction roads". Though intended primarily for timber lorries, these roads are open to the public for walking, and the occasional slow moving traffic on them does nothing to detract from the pleasure of those seeking a tranquil retreat from the noise and danger of the public roads.

Trees to be felled, either as a thinning or final clearance of a plantation, are measured and marked by the foresters. The marking is usually a dot with white paint at about four feet above ground and trees thus indicated are then offered for sale by tender, prospective purchasers being supplied with a list showing numbers, species, measurements and estimated volume of each sale lot.

Felling is done by axe, cross-cut or chain-saw. After trimming of all side branches, the stems are dragged by horse or tractor to the loading point on a forest road where they may be cut into sections before transport by lorry to sawmill or industrial plant— pulp, chipboard or wallboard manufacturing.

Although only a fraction of Irish State Forests are yielding timber, most are still too young for thinning or final clearance before replanting, the annual production is considerable. It amounted to nearly 300,000 tons in recent years, bringing in a revenue of £1½ million.

This sum was the amount paid by merchants for the trees in the forests. When they were felled and transported to sawmill and factory they were worth much more and when turned into sawn boards, chipboard, wallboard and paper the value went up to about £10 million, most of the material going to the home market but an increasing quantity being exported each year.

Chapter III

THE FACE OF IRELAND

The principal mountain ranges and the rocks of which they are formed; soil, bogs, sand dunes; the larger rivers and man-made alterations to the country.

In Ireland we have a wide diversity of topography due to differences in geography, geology and the effect of the Ice Age. The mountains, the rocks of which they are formed, their soil covering and the soils of the lowlands vary from district to district and have a fundamental influence on our scenery.

A little knowledge of the physical structure of our island adds greatly to the interest of a country journey. The rocks which form the mountains and underlie the soils of the plains are well worth a study. There are over twenty different sorts of rock in Ireland all of which give a distinctive character to the district where they occur. The Geological Map published in 1962 shows their location in colours on a scale of 1 inch = 12 miles. Here can be seen the great Central Plain of "good land" underlain by limestone and extending from Lough Neagh to Fermoy with arms reaching to the sea at Dublin, Galway and Sligo. Antrim and part of Derry are peculiar in their foundation of Basalt, a volcanic rock covering almost the entire county of Antrim. The Mountains of Mourne, like the Wicklow Mountains, the hills bordering on the north coast of Galway Bay and the Derryveagh range in Donegal are of Granite, a soft rock which crumbles easily to give a rounded outline contrasting with the craggy shapes of the Quartzite seen in the Sugar Loaf in Wicklow, Forth Mountain in Wexford, Maamturk and the Twelve Bens in Connemara, Nephin Beg in Mayo and many of the peaks of Donegal extending from Killybegs through

65

"The Lakes of Killarney", now a National Park, are the centre piece of a world famous beauty spot since the days of stage coaches. Seen from a boat there is an ever changing vista of mountains and woods, glinting waterfalls, islands ablaze with sub-tropical flowers and romantic castles and abbeys. Arbutus, a Mediterranean shrub, grows naturally here, a survivor of Ireland's pre-Ice Age flora which escaped in the general glaciation of the rest of the country. The MacGillycuddy Reeks with Carrantoohil 3,414 feet, our highest mountain, are a few miles to the west.

Gweedore to Carndonagh in the peninsula of Innisowen between the Swilly and the Foyle. Another widespread rock formation is Red Sandstone which is found in the Slieve Bloom range in Laois and Offaly, in the Slieve Aughty on the Clare-Galway border, in the lower levels of the Galtees and the hills of North Tipperary and Limerick and occurring in an almost continuous mass from Kilmacthomas in County Waterford westwards till it meets the Atlantic Ocean off the coast of Kerry. In this span it forms the backbone of the mountains which comprise the "Munster

Barrier", that chain of highland which includes the Comeragh, the Monavullagh, the Knockmealdown, Nagles' Mountain, Boggeragh, Shehy, Derrynasaggart, Caha and the Macgillicuddy Reeks of Co. Kerry. Small areas of Red Sandstone are found north of Boyle, west of Castlebar and near Castlerea and a larger one between Lower Lough Erne and Lough Neagh. A shale type of rock underlies much of East and West Wicklow, a major part of Wexford and it forms the Sheffrey Hills to the west of Lough Mask in Co. Mayo. Shale is also the foundation rock of the area stretching from Newtownards through Banbridge to Drogheda, Kells and Newtown Forbes near the town of Longford. "Coal Measures", a term covering the series of coal seams with clay, sandstone and shale, extends northwards from Killarney through

Sybil Point and the Three Sisters near Smerwick on the Dingle Peninsula. A few miles to the south in Blasket Sound lies the sunken ship Santa Maria de la Rosa said to be carrying some of the gold bullion of the Spanish Arada. It struck a rock and was wrecked in 1588 and the Admiral and 500 crew and soldiers were drowned in these stormy seas. Diving in search of the gold is being done at present.

the Mullaghareirk Mountains into Co. Clare. It occurs again in the hills between Carlow and Castlecomer, in a small area of the Slieveardagh near Killenaule and around Lough Allen in Co. Leitrim, which are all centres of coal mining.

These are some of the important rock formations which form the "foundation" of our island. In places they show on the surface; on craggy hill tops, especially those formed of quartzite, and in the dramatic Limestone "pavements" of the Burren in North Clare and in the Aran Islands. Nearly everywhere, however, the rock is covered with a layer of soil or of peat which lies deeply in the plains and diminishes in thickness as its ascends the hills.

Soil is a highly complex material formed of grains of broken down rocks in mixture with humus resulting from decayed vegetation and containing the nutrients on which plant life and ultimately all life on earth depends. As well as the chemical nutrients— Phosphate, Potash, Nitrates and Lime are the chief—the soil to be fertile must have certain bacteria and fungi, micro-organisms as the soil scientists call them, as well, of course, as water and air. Too much or too little of any one of the necessary things results in a poor soil capable of supporting only certain plants or, in extreme cases, a completely barren soil.

Soil can consist of fragments of the rocks immediately underlying it but in nearly all cases it has been transported and is made up of a variety of material from far-away places. It may have been carried by water and deposited as "alluvium" along the courses of rivers, but is more likely to have resulted from ice action many thousands of years ago. During the "Ice Age" Ireland and

Top left:
For sixty miles from Larne to Portstewart the Antrim Coast Road skirts the sea, linking Glenarm, Carnlough, Cushendall, Ballycastle and Portrush, and affording views of the Basaltic columns of the Giant's Causeway and Rathlin Island. It was built as a famine relief work at the foot of the cliffs which tower over the sea except where interrupted by the "Glens of Antrim".

Bottom left:
The district around Cushendall is the only part of Co. Antrim underlain by Granite and Red Sandstone. with a sheltered bay and seaside amenities. In the neighbourhood there are caverns hollowed by the waves from the Sandstone cliffs.

In St. George's Channel a few miles off Carnsore Point is
the Tuskar Rock with its lighthouse. Many migrating birds
are attracted by the light or land exhausted on the rock. The
lighthouse was built in 1913 and its light is visible for 19 miles
at sea. All the lighthouses around our coasts are maintained
by the Commissioners of Irish Lights.

Top left·
A few miles north of Cushendall is the seaside resort and bay
of Cushendun intersected by the coast road which climbs the
cliffs at Torr Head and looks across the narrow North Channel
to Scotland. The village was designed by a Welsh architect
and rebuilt before the First World War and was acquired a
few years ago by the National Trust as "a perfect example of
an Ulster seaside village". It is in the centre of the Glens of
Antrim.

Bottom left:
Upper and Lower Lough Erne cover 30,000 acres and divide
Fermanagh into two and a trip through them by water or
lake shore provides 50 miles of unspoilt rural scenery. The
lakes are the basin of the River Erne which rises in the
southern part of Cavan and expands into the Upper Lough,
seen in the picture above near Knockninney, contracting at
the point where the bridge crosses at Enniskillen and then
expanding into the large Lower Lough. At the outlet near
Belleek the waters again contract into a narrow river which
operates the Erne Hydroelectric station near Ballyshannon.

71

Northern Europe were covered by a sheet of ice and snow which lay hundreds of feet deep over the land. With the advent of warmer conditions a thaw started in the south and as the southern ice melted the sheet of ice broke up into massive avalanches which slid southwards. As it travelled it melted and formed "glacial rivers" which deposited boulders, gravel, sand and finer particles of rock that today form the mineral part of our soils. The ice movement ground and scored the mountains in its path and in Cork, Kerry, Galway and other places the direction of travel can be made out from the scrapes still visible on bare rock.

One series of deposited soils resulted from the melting of local ice which carried material from neighbouring hills to the plains beneath. Another, and more important, series was due to the mass movement of Northern ice from Scotland and farther afield. This scoured the bed of the North Channel and the Irish Sea and

Lough Gill in Co. Sligo is associated with the poet W. B Yeats who wrote the poem "The Lake Isle of Innisfree" about a little island not far from Church Island shown below.

Mullingar, "a citadel which menaced and oftentimes laid waste to the territories of the ancient Irish chieftains and was as frequently plundered and burned by the avenging foe" at one period but nowadays a thriving market town and a centre of the beef raising industry. Mullingar, like most large Irish towns until recently held monthly cattle fairs in the main street, a purpose admirably suited by its great width. Lough Owel and Ennel, famous for dapping for lake trout with live May flies as bait, are nearby.

deposited a deep and rich layer over our midland and eastern region. Evidence of this ice movement is provided by pieces of pink coloured granite, "Ailsa Craig Granite", which is peculiar to that sentinel rock which stands guard at the exit from the Firth of Clyde and which are to be found in the clay cliffs between Killiney and Bray and in the gravel pits of Kilquade and other parts of east Co. Wicklow. Other reminders of the Ice Age are the thousands of lakes formed in depressions left by the glacial rivers, in the "dry gaps" such as The Scalp and Glen of the Downs torn through mountain barriers by these rivers, and by "erratics", which are rocks foreign to the district in which they now lie and traceable to a northern source.

73

Two Irish words are internationally used for features resulting from the Ice Age—Drumlin and Esker. Drumlins are low hog-backed mounds of soil, commonly 50 to 100 feet in height and several hundred yards long. They are a prominent feature of the country which extends westwards from Carrickmacross over Monaghan, Cavan and Leitrim to South Donegal, forming steep sided hills of mostly heavy clay soils, Eskers are common in many parts of the country, and compose the great ridge across the Midlands which carried one of the five roads to Tara. They are mounds of gravel left by streams of melted ice and were formed at a point where a glacier was halted by a hill, lake or the sea. Here the debris of gravel and sand carried by the ice is left in a continuous chain along the edge of the ice sheet.

Bog is another Irish word with world-wide usage. One type is formed by an accumulation of plant remains in shallow lakes and consists of a spongy mass of half decayed vegetation with a surface growth of Sphagnum and other swamp species. These are the High Bogs of Basin Peats—called "High" because their surface rises above the level of the surrounding land. They are extensive, the Bog of Allen goes from mid Kildare through Offaly and across the Shannon south of Athlone into East Galway and has arms extending over Laois and reaching to near Cashel in Co. Tipperary. Basin bogs also occur in North-east Cork, in Kerry, Connemara, Roscommon, Mayo and in parts of Derry and Antrim. There are also the Blanket Bogs of the mountains, continuous covers of peat which follow the contours of the ground, resulting from the partial decay of mosses and other plants in a cool, damp climate and over an acid underlying rock and forming a layer which is usually shallow on knolls and deeper in dips in the ground. The Blanket Bogs are found on all our high mountains—the "Feather Bed" in the Dublin Mountains is the start of an extensive tract which reaches to Baltinglass at the southern end of the Wicklow Mountains. The Comeragh Range in Waterford, the Boggeragh, the Mullaghareirk, Derrynasaggart, and the Reeks of Cork and Kerry,

Left:
The giant pylons of the E.S.B. stride across the land bringing electricity to light our homes and power our factories and farms. Modern living depends more and more on electricity and the E.S.B. uses many sources of power to generate it. There are water operated stations on the Shannon, Liffey, Lee and Erne, turf burning stations at Portarlington, Lanesboro, Bellacorick and other places, a native coal fired one at Lough Allen and large oil burning ones in Dublin, Cork and Little Island near Waterford. An unusual type is being built at Turlough Hill in Wicklow—it will pump up water at night and use it during the day to meet peak loads.

west Galway, Mayo, Sligo, Leitrim, Donegal, Tyrone and Antrim have stretches of bog of thicknesses from a few inches up to several feet.

An interesting phenomenon is the presence of pine timber, "Bog Deal", which is uncovered during turf harvesting. This is the remains of trees of the same species as our present day "Scots" Pine which formed vast forests before 550 B.C. Later the climate became wetter, windier and decidedly cooler, the bog on which the trees stood became swampy and the peat began to grow and in time killed the pines. Storms uprooted them and the prostrate trunks were submerged and preserved from decay by the peat which continued to grow in depth until it covered the fallen pine trees to a depth of feet.

And now, a short look at our Irish rivers; great and small their courses are places of great beauty and they traverse some of the best land and the most populous regions of our country.

The wide estuary of Waterford Harbour receives the "Three Sisters" which rise within a few miles of each other in the Slieve Bloom and Devil's Bit ranges. The most northerly of the three, the Barrow, flows through flat land to Portarlington, Athy and southwards to Carlow and it meets no high ground until at Graiguenamanagh it reaches a deep gorge which extends to New

Trees and flowering plants border the River Dargle in the Glen between Bray and the Powerscourt Waterfall.

Ross where it is joined by the Nore. This river comes down through Kilkenny, Ballyragget and Thomastown, by the wooded slopes of Inistiogue and Desertmore to its junction at Ballyanne. The third "sister", the Suir, takes a more westerly course than the other two and passes Templemore, Thurles and Golden before turning south to Cahir and Ardfinnan from where it skirts the high ground to Clonmel and follows the base of the Comeraghs to Carrick-on-Suir and the city of Waterford.

Left:

A bog pool in Co. Mayo with the stumps of pine trees which grew many thousands of years ago when the climate was warmer and drier than it is now. Bad weather set in about 500 B.C. the bog mosses grew and the peat level was raised and gradually covered and killed the trees. The stumps and any prostrate trees were preserved by the bog water. The leaves of Water Lilies float on the surface. This is probably the white flowered species which prefers a peaty bottom for growth.

The Liffey rises on the western slopes of Kippure and after wandering seventy miles through Poulaphuca, Newbridge, Leixlip and Lucan it meets the sea at Dublin only thirteen miles from its source. Geologists tell us that its original course was a short one through the Slade of Saggart at Brittas but that its passage was blocked by glacial drift which caused a diversion to its present lengthy route. On it are water-powered electric stations at Poulaphuca and at Leixlip.

The Boyne comes from Kildare to Trim and Navan where it is joined by the northern Blackwater which flows southwards from Co. Cavan through Kells and traverses the beautiful "Boyne Valley" by Slane and passes near the ancient tumuli of New Grange, Dowth and Knowth to Drogheda and the sea near Mornington.

Another Leinster river is the Slaney, rising on Lugnaquilla above Glen Imaal and flowing through Stratford, Baltinglass, Tullow and the mountain pass near Bunclody down to Enniscorthy and the sea just short of Wexford town.

The southern Blackwater is regarded as the most beautiful of Irish rivers. It passes through picturesque country from its source in the Derrynasaggart Mountains by the Boggeragh and Mullaghareirk ranges to Banteer and Mallow; thence it flows between wooded hill slopes to Fermoy, Lismore, Cappoquin down to the sea in Youghal Bay.

The Lee in its short course from Gougane Barra to Inchageelagh and to the artificial lake and hydro-electric station below Macroom passes through lovely country until it flows into Cork Harbour. The Bandon rises near Dunmanway and flows to Enniskean and Bandon and on to Kinsale Harbour. The overland portion of the Roughty or Kenmare river is insignificant—its magnificence is in the 30 mile long estuary which reaches from Kenmare between the Caha and the MacGillycuddy Reeks to the Atlantic Ocean.

The Shannon is the longest river in Great Britain and Ireland. It's route is 170 miles from its source in the "Shannon Pot" on the slopes of Cuilcagh to Loughs Allen, Ree and Derg, by the towns of Carrick-on-Shannon, Lanesboro, Athlone, Banagher, Portumna, Killaloe to Limerick. It is a navigable river widely used for pleasure boats and, until recently, for commercial transport as part of the Grand Canal system. The first major hydro-electric station, the "Shannon Scheme", was built on this river at Ardnacrusha above Limerick, and below Limerick is the transatlantic Shannon Airport. The estuary is longer than that of

The glens of East Wicklow, Glencree, Glenmacanass, Glenda-lough, Glenmalure are renowned beauty spots. On a smaller scale is the Dargle Glen, 2 miles from Bray, which has been planted as a woodland garden with rare trees and shrubs which add interest to its natural charm.

the Kenmare River and reaches for 60 miles between Counties Clare, Limerick and Kerry to the open Atlantic at Loop Head.

Connemara is severed from the rest of Galway by Lough Corrib, a 25 mile stretch which narrows into the Corrib River where it enters the bay at Galway city. The Moy in Co. Mayo carries the waters of Lough Conn and Lough Cullin by Foxford and Ballina to the sea at Killala Bay. A trio of streams, the Owenbeg, the Owenmore and the Unshin meet at Coolooney and continue as the Ballysodare River to Ballysodare Bay.

The River Erne rises in Co. Cavan and when it has crossed into Co. Fermanagh it swells into an intricate mesh of lakes and islands to form the 50 mile long Lough Erne which again narrows to enter Co. Donegal and the sea at Ballyshannon. The principal town on the lough is Enniskillen between the Upper and Lower Loughs. There is a hydro-electric station at the outlet from the Lower Lough.

Two large rivers have their outlets on the north coast—the Foyle which flows into Lough Foyle at Derry, and the Bann near Coleraine on the Antrim-Derry boundary. The Foyle is the con-fluence of several streams from the Sperrins and the mountains of East Donegal which together flow into the 40 miles long lough from near Strabane to the open sea at Inisowen Head. The Bann rises in Co. Down and makes its way by Portadown to Lough Neagh, a vast inland sea in the heart of Northern Ireland and continues as the Lower Bann through Toombridge, Portglenone and Coleraine to the sea at Lough Foyle. The Lagan rises in the hills of Co. Down and goes by way of Dromore, Lisburn and Belfast to its estuary in Belfast Lough.

The entire coastline of Ireland with all its bays and inlets comes to about 2,000 miles. We are fortunate in that it is largely still unspoilt although subjected to increasing pressure for housing, recreation and industrial development. Majestic cliffs are common all around the coast but for recreation and amenity the most appealing feature is the abundance of sand dunes and sandy beaches. The former cover about 34,000 acres and their proximity to the sea, the clean dry nature of the sand and the shelter afforded by the little hillocks makes them favourite places for the camper, caravanner and picnicker. The dunes result from the accumulation

Downhill in the centre of the six mile sweep of Magilligan Strand on Lough Foyle, north of Derry, not far from Castlerock, is noted for its variety of sea shells, as many as 118 different kinds have been picked up in one day. The eccentric Earl of Bristol when Bishop of Derry in 1783 built the Mussenden Temple on the cliff top.

*The source of the River Lee is in Gougane Barra Lake
situated in an amphitheatre of steep cliffs down which many
streams cascade. On an island is the ruins of St. Finbarr's
Church which is a place of pilgrimage. The Forest Park in
the glen has a "ring road" with wonderful views over the
Shehy Mountains and down the valley towards Inchageelagh.*

by wind of fine grit formed by wave action on the beach and then
blown to the rim of the coast where it is stabilised to a limited
extent by Marram grass and other plants. Very often the dunes
block the natural outlet for rivers to the sea and their hinterland
is a swampy marsh as a result.

The actions of man over thousands of years have affected the
look of our country. First came the clearance of the native woods
to make way for grazing and tillage. The 17th and 18th centuries
saw the enclosure of land by fences, ditches, hedges and walls,
the removal of surface rocks which impeded ploughs and the
drainage of wet areas. Roads were constructed and houses built on
farms, in villages and towns. Foreign trees were brought in and
were widely planted in parks and residential demesnes. Canals

and railways were constructed and in more recent times modern transport demanded airports and motor roads.

The division of the country into farms brought the greatest change. At first these were homesteads with a "bawn" or stockade where cattle and other animals spent the night safe from thieves and wolves. There were few fields and the farm animals roamed the open country except for a few areas fenced for tillage. By degrees more land was enclosed, roads and tracks were defined and the country assumed its present pattern. The 18th century was the great age of land improvement. "Improving landlords" brought in efficient iron ploughs and other farm implements which were far superior to the crude ones of timber generally in use; they adopted better practices of cropping with superior strains of seed and they imported improved breeds of cattle and sheep. Labour was plentiful and the levelling of land, ditch building, draining, liming and marling were carried out by gangs of spademen, "spalpeens" who travelled the country. The landed pro-

Near Tralee Bay are the Magharee Islands, known as "The Seven Hogs", one of which, Illauntannig, has the remains of an early Christian Monastery.

prietors vied with each other in building fine mansions and in landscaping the surroundings by constructing avenues, damming streams to form lakes and by tree planting. This last left a permanent mark on our scenery. An Irish view today in almost any part of the country shows groves, avenues and hedgerows of spreading hardwood trees, many of foreign species, all due to the fashion started two centuries ago.

In the heart of the pleasant farmlands of East Galway the Tynagh Mines herald the start of mining operations which will affect the appearance of many parts of our country. Harvesting goes on within yards of the concentrator plant and Mallard Duck and Seagulls nest on the nearby artificial dam.

This mine at Tynagh and the ones at Silvermines, Gortrim and Avoca in 1970 produced a total of nearly 350 million tons of Lead, Zinc and Copper concentrates, valued at over £18 million.

The operators plan to restore and landscape the surface of areas mined when the work is finished.

Chapter IV

WILD LIFE IN WOODS, FIELDS, MOUNTAINS, BOGS, SEASHORE LAKES AND STREAMS

The Birds and other wild animals, insects and plants which are to be seen in country places

LIFE in the countryside, or even a day's visit, is much more rewarding for those with a knowledge of the birds, beasts and plants which they come across. Of these, the birds are undoubtedly of greatest interest to most people. Nearly four hundred different species of birds have been seen in Ireland at one time or another but only a hundred of these are "resident", that is birds which remain with us the whole year round, building their nests and rearing their young. Others, such as the Wild Geese, are Winter immigrants which come here in the Autumn to escape the cold of their northern homes and depart in the Spring, or, like the Swallows, are Summer immigrants which spend the warm months of the year with us and move south when cold weather sets in. Still others are merely birds of passage which land here in the course of a journey, possibly accidentally as a result of being blown off course by a gale, or to fortify themselves with food and drink before continuing to their destination.

Not everyone will want to become an enthusiastic "bird watcher" who with his binoculars will lie for hours in a "hide" in order to get a brief glance at a rare species, but most people like to be able to name the common birds. Probably the most common of all is the Blackbird. This is a true resident, breeding in all parts of Ireland, but it is also an immigrant, immense numbers flying in

*Is a long neck an advantage? This Cock Blackbird seems to
be trying to drop a grub into the open beak of the smallest
triplet but big brothers are not going to be overlooked.
It is a native species—the legend of Oisin tells of the warrior's
delight in the sweet song of the Blackbird. Food is worms,
slugs, snails and insects, berries of all kinds and fruit—
gardeners know how partial it is to red strawberries and ripe
apples. The nest is mud lined like a thrush's but has an
inner layer of dry grass.*

every winter from the continent of Europe, banished by the harsh weather. Another widespread resident is the Wren, augmented in Winter time by small flocks of continental immigrants. Our Song Thrush is a bit of a traveller—it nests in Ireland, goes off at the end of July to foreign parts and comes back again during the winter, it is thought in February. Some Robins are wholly resident; others migrate southwards in Winter. Blue Tits behave in much the same manner, some staying all the year, some leaving in the autumn, and in addition there is some evidence that foreign tits arrive in October to remain until spring.

These are all species which are found in suburban gardens. Out in the more open spaces of the fields they occur too, together with many other kinds which it takes the hunger of a harsh Winter to drive near to human habitations. The Common Rook, or Crow as it is generally called in Ireland, is very much a bird of the farm-

The little Blue Titmouse is one of the best known of our native birds, frequenting gardens, hedgerows and woodlands. It is a voracious creature and eats enormous quantities of green fly and other insects—it is fond of cream and is adept at piercing the metal tops of milk bottles. It nests in hollows in trees and walls and will readily occupy a nesting box put up for its use.

lands where it lives on grubs and grain, potatoes and anything else it can pick up. Another common species is the Starling, like the Crow given to living in great flocks. Both species are increased in number by autumn migrations of foreign birds. Chaffinches, Bullfinches, Linnets, Skylarks, Pied Wagtails, Hedge Sparrows are frequently to be seen out in the fields. Bogs and swampy places are the haunts of Snipe and Lapwing, and where there is a lake, of Duck of many kinds. Sea-coast marshes provide the wintering ground for vast flocks of Geese which come from Greenland in

Top right:

"Hail to thee, blithe Spirit!
Bird thou never wert,
That from heaven, or near it,
Pourest thy full heart
In profuse strains of unpremeditated art"
wrote the poet Shelley of the Skylark soaring into the clouds and showering down "a rain of melody".
This small, brown bird is a native. Food consists of insects, worms and seeds.

Bottom right:
The Pied Wagtail goes about in a series of short, quick runs; it is said to be the smallest bird which actually can walk, other small birds only hop. It lives on insects found in fields or about water and builds its nest in a cleft in a cliff, bank or wall. It is native but there is much coming and going between Ireland and the Continent.

→ — [OVERLEAF]
"I'll protect you!" The Cob, or Male Swan stands guard over the Penn on her nest beside the lake in Oakpark, Carlow. They resent intruders at nesting time and taking this close-up picture put the photographer in some peril.
The Common or Mute Swan is claimed as a true Irish native, the ancient legend tells us that the Children of Lir were changed into swans, but in England they credit King Richard I with bringing it from Cyprus on his triumphal return from the Crusades. It breeds on lakes and rivers all over Ireland and is seen on the seashore and in estuaries. It feeds on vegetable matter which it dredges out of the water and will eat grain.
The young are called Cygnets and are sooty grey without any of the magnificence of their parents (hence the tale of the "Ugly Duckling"). When small they ride on the mother's back as she sails over the water.

90

The Wild Duck builds its nest near the water sheltered under reeds or other plants. It is made of dry grass and lined with downy feathers. When she is leaving the nest, the duck covers the eggs with bits of grass if she is given time— the duck who owned this nest left in a hurry.

Top right:
The Common Wild Duck or Mallard is the stock from which domestic ducks are descended. It is a migratory bird and large flocks arrive here in October. The picture shows two which were captured on the North Slob Wildfowl Refuge in Wexford. Some remain over the summer and nest along the shores of lakes and rivers.
The drakes are rich glossy green on head and neck with snowy white collars and black curls on their tails. The ducks are brown.

Bottom right:
A Whooper Swan from Iceland arriving at its winter quarters in Ireland. These large birds, five feet from the tip of the yellow bill to the tail, breed in Ireland on the shores and islands of small lakes and tundra, and about 2,000 spend the winter here mostly in fresh water lakes and on large rivers. In flight their wing-beats are silent unlike the Common Wild Swan, the Mute Swan, which makes a loud swishing sound.

The Gannet is a large bird, nearly 3 feet long, found in rocky parts of the coast where it feeds on herrings and other fish of which it eats an enormous quantity. A flock of gannets feeding is a sure sign to fishermen that a shoal of herrings is there. There are colonies on Little Skellig, off the Kerry coast, one of the few islands where it breeds, shown in picture.

Close-up of colony of Gannets on Little Skellig—the most southerly nesting place of this bird in Ireland.

October to remain until April, mainly along our eastern coast, from Wexford to Co. Down. The coast, indeed, is the best place to see a variety of birds. Here, on the rim of the ocean will be found Gulls, Oyster Catchers, Wild Duck, Cormorant, Gannet and many other water birds, both residents and migrants. On rivers and inland water there are Herons, known to country people as Cranes, and Swans, Dippers and, rarely seen, the beautiful little Kingfishers.

All woodlands, especially those of mixed species including Oak, Beech and other deciduous broadleaved trees, are the favourite haunt of many birds for nesting, roosting and sanctuary even if the woods themselves may not provide much food. Wood pigeons are numerous, Jays, Tree Creepers, Great Tits, Woodcock, Chiffchaff are all found.

Of game birds the Pheasant is the most conspicuous with its bright colours of yellow, red and blue. It was brought into Ireland about 400 years ago and it is artificially reared for shooting on many estates but wild pheasants are seen in all parts of the country where there are a few bushes and trees to provide cover.

On the heather moors Grouse are found, especially where their

The black and white Oyster Catchers are common around our coast and flocks like this one at Greystones will be seen skimming along the shore or lighting in the sea. It feeds on mussels, whelks and limpets which are scooped from their shells by the birds' beak.

95

The domestic and the pigeon seen in city streets are descended from the Blue Rock pigeon which nests in rocky places. It varies greatly in colour and appearance and pigeon fanciers have bred Pouter, Fantail, Nun and other odd looking birds. Above is a flock of pigeons at Sandymount.

96

Sparrowhawks inhabit wooded areas where they flit rapidly through the trees and dart along hedges with eyes fast moving as they search for their prey. They are crabbed and pugnacious and will attack and kill pigeons, magpies and other birds much larger than themselves, as well as rats, mice and frogs.

The picture is of a Hen Sparrowhawk on her nest. She is greyish white in front and is larger than the greyish brown male—hens confined in cages have been known to attack and eat their mates.

Small birds will occasionally gang-up in flocks to drive a sparrowhawk from their locality.

enemies Grey Crows and Magpies which feed on the eggs and young birds are kept down in numbers. Grouse live on young shoots of heather and a well managed moorland has strips of old heather burnt over at intervals of a few years to encourage the growth of fresh succulent shoots.

There are a number of books on birds. "Ireland's Birds" by R. F. Ruttledge tells of their distribution and migrations. A "Manual of British Birds" by H. Saunders with illustrations, describes their appearance and habits. The National Museum, Dublin, publishes a list of Irish Birds with their frequency and habitats.

The Common Tern is found on the coast and inland on many
lakes. It is a migrant, arriving in April for nesting and usually
departing before the end of October. The adults have orange-
red beaks, black heads and neck, back pearl grey and front
white. They feed on small fish, eels, shrimps and insects.
The picture is of Roseate Terns in Co. Wexford. This breed is
a rare summer visitor and there are nesting colonies in only
a few spots. It has a black beak, the back is a paler grey than
the common tern and the front has a slight pink tinge through
the white.

Top right:
Is he wise or is it the fluffy head feathers which give the
appearance of a bewigged judge delivering the verdict of the
court? This Long-eared Owl is a nestling having his first
journey from home and not pleased with the photographer
and his camera. It is a native bird, living in plantations and
hunting at night for mice, rats, small birds and beetles. It
makes a "quacking" noise when flying or when perched and
occasionally hoots.

Bottom right:
Wherever there are houses there will certainly be House
Sparrows living in colonies in ivy covered walls and garden
bushes and keeping up a loud chattering as they fly about
foraging for insects and larvae and anything they can pick up
in the way of grain and other food—here is a Cock House
Sparrow enjoying a meal of bread crumbs.

98

Most of our common animals have been introduced from abroad, including all our domestic ones—the horse, ass, cow, sheep, dog, cat and even rats and mice. Native wild animals are the Red Deer, a magnificent creature found in Kerry, Wicklow and Donegal, the Badger, Fox, Red Squirrel, Stoat (usually referred to as a Weasel), Otter and Hare, all widely distributed. The last Irish Wolf was killed in Co. Carlow in 1786; the breed is said to have been exceptionally ferocious and as "large as a young horse".

Fallow Deer were introduced and are now our most common species of deer. The Normans brought in the Rabbit which was a serious pest to farmers and foresters for many centuries until in recent years it was greatly reduced in numbers by disease.

A useful book on mammals is "History of British Mammals" by G. Barrett-Hamilton.

There is an immense variety of smaller creatures, insects and spiders, which are met in the countryside. Of the latter there are 327 different species! Butterflies are the most conspicuous of insects. The commonest are the Large White, Small White, Tortoiseshell, well-known from its habit of hibernating indoors, Peacock, Red Admiral, Meadow Brown, Common Blue and Silver

Top left:
The Stag or Red Deer is an Irish species still found in the Wicklow and Galtee Mountains, in Killarney and in Glenveigh in Co. Donegal. It is the largest species of deer, up to 4 feet high at the shoulders, and is a warm reddish brown colour in summer turning grey in winter. The much branched antlers, unlike those of the Fallow Deer, have round blades.
The Red Deer are fast runners and great swimmers, having been known to swim for 6 miles. They live mainly on grass but will browse on leaves of trees and brambles.

Bottom left:
Fallow Deer were brought to Ireland by the Normans and at one time were in "Deer Parks" on estates all over the country, and are still fairly numerous in forest areas. They are up to 3 feet high at the shoulders and range in colour from light to dark brown, sometimes dappled and with white lines. The antlers grow annually, appearing as velvet covered knobs in spring, developing into hard bony structures in autumn and falling off every winter. Their size and number of points show the age of the deer.
The picture shows deer in the Phoenix Park.

101

No one knows when the rabbit was brought to Ireland. It has been here for hundreds of years and was very plentiful until recently when it was nearly wiped out by a disease, Myxomatosis. Rabbits are prolific animals and a single pair could produce 11 million descendants in three years if all lived. Their food is grass and young plants of all sorts and they do serious damage by stripping the bark and biting the tops off small trees.
Rabbits live in burrows in ditches and sandy places.

Top right:
Lizards like sunning themselves on a warm rock. They are nimble creatures and are very hard to catch. Never grab them by the tail as it will come off! They feed on insects and snails. Their young are born alive and not hatched from eggs as with other reptiles, hence the name "vivaparous".

Bottom right:
Toads are not natives of Ireland—this fellow is in Dublin Zoo. They are like frogs in looks but are squatter and have many warts and protuberances on the skin. Frogs feed on insects, spiders and worms, toads prefer slugs, snails, worms and beetles.

Otters live on river banks in dry crevices and feed on fish. They are covered in brown fur and are up to 40 inches in length. In some countries they are trained to catch and retrieve fish.

◆—[OVERLEAF]
Wild Goats on Dalkey Island perched on a hill of granite rock still scored and rounded by the passage of ice over it many thousands of years ago. These goats are the same as the common domestic goat which is kept in Ireland for its milk and in other countries for meat as well. Kid gloves are made from the skin of young goats.
If a goat attacks, the thing to do is to catch it by the beard!

The Chaffinch is one of the commonest of our native birds and the residents are augmented in late autumn by large numbers of immigrants. It is called the "Bachelor Bird" because the cocks leave the hens at the end of the summer and spend the winter in large all-male flocks until the next nesting season in April. They live on insects and small seeds.

Fritillary. Species of Moths are more numerous than Butterflies, but as they are mostly nocturnal flyers they are less noticeable. There are a couple of dozen species of Dragon Fly, and large numbers of different Bees, Wasps, Flies, Cockroaches, Centipedes and Millipedes.

For a study of insects the illustrated "Oxford Book of Insects" by J. Burton, published by Oxford University Press in 1968 is recommended.

Wild plants may be included amongst the "Wild Life" interests of the countryside. There are over a thousand species of native plants to be found in fields, woods, bogs and mountains, by lake and seashore and along the course of streams and rivers. Not all are flowering plants—there are many grasses, mosses and inconspicuous plants—but the following short list are worth knowing as they are of singular beauty when in flower: Poppy, Purple

Wildflowers on Slea Head at the extremity of the Dingle Peninsula, the most westerly point in Europe.
There are few plants on this wild, wind-swept area and visitors should refrain from collecting even the most common. There is much else to see in this remote spot—it is rich in pre-Christian and early Christian remains. West of Ventry are forts, raths, crosses, inscribed stones, souterrains and hundreds of stone bee-hive huts.

Top left:
The wonder of the Dandelion! Every small seed on its head is furnished with a parachute so that the wind may carry it to new ground away from the mother plant.
It is one of the commonest of plants in meadows, pastures and waste places and occurs from sea level to high on mountains.
Children get fun blowing the grey seed-heads to "tell the time"—it is nearly midnight by this one!

Bottom left:
Pipewort or to give it its botanical name, Jointed Eriocaulon, is found growing in marshy places in the West of Ireland. The rootstock creeps in the mud and sends up to the surface tufts of narrow pointed leaves and heads composed of many small greyish flowers carried on stalks up to 3 feet long when the water is deep. It avoids limestone.

109

Seals are mammals, bearing live young and nurturing them on milk during their early months. They are numerous around the coast feeding on fish which they pursue with great speed and coming on land to sun themselves on the warm rocks of the seashore. Seal skins are valuable and large numbers of these animals are killed each year for their pelts.

Loosestrife, Bluebell, Ragged Robin, Wood Anemone, Primrose, Cowslip, Water Forget-me-not, Foxglove, Wood Sorrel, Marsh Marigold, Wild Rose, Fumitory, Rose Willow Herb.

Authoritative books on the subject are "Cybele Hibernica" by More & Colgan, "The Botanist in Ireland" by R. L. Praeger and "Natural History of Ireland" by the same author. A popular book is "The Concise British Flora in Colour" by Keble Martin published by Sphere Books Ltd., Gray's Inn Road, London, W.C.1.

Chapter V

COUNTRY PURSUITS

Walking, and what may be seen in fields, woods and mountains. Adventure sports, horse riding, caravanning, sailing; visiting historic houses, fine parks and gardens, ancient castles and monasteries

THE open spaces of the countryside make possible a great number of activities which are more and more sought in this age of reduced working hours and long week-ends. The population of towns and cities desire to get away from the confinement of the streets into the broad expanses of mountain and forest, seashore and river and to avail of the pursuits which are open to them.

A popular one is walking; walking for the pleasure of exercise and to get near to the life of the country which is missed by faster methods of travel. There are many thousands of miles of unfrequented roads and lanes, and for those who wish to get away from all danger of motor cars, there are the roads through State Forests and uncharted tracks across the hills. In these latter cases walkers should take care not to start forest or heather fires nor to disturb game birds by bringing uncontrolled dogs. An Oige, 39 Mountjoy Square, Dublin 1 provides a large number of hostels for the use of youthful hikers. Bryson House, Bedford St., Belfast will give information about youth hostels in Northern Ireland.

Walking can be combined with the study of field botany, birds, animals, and insects. There is a host of books on natural history, some like the excellent "I Spy" series of coloured picture booklets on country subjects such as "In the Wood", "Trees" and "Wild Flowers" published by The Dickens Press at a very reasonable price, up to expensive scientific books. A useful one on trees and

111

*Shooting the rapids on the River Liffey. Canoeing is a thrilling
sport open to young people on our many fine rivers—it is
reasonably inexpensive and, with commonsense, quite safe.*

*The country can be crossed by canoe from Dublin by canal
and Lough Derg to the Atlantic at the Shannon's mouth, or
through the Barrow Navigation canal to New Ross and the
estuary of the "Three Sisters" below Waterford. Another
cross-country trip is via the Northern Blackwater into Lough
Neagh and down the Lower Bann to the sea near Coleraine.*

Top left:

*In the Mourne Mountains the sea is very near, lapping to
their feet all the way from Rostrevor to Newcastle. They are
kindly mountains, never oppressing by their height, although
the tallest is 2,800 feet, and the towns, Warrenpoint, Hilltown,
Kilkeel and Castlewellan are conveniently spaced for walkers
and cyclists.*

Bottom left:

*An Oige Hostel at Kinvara, Co. Galway, sheltered from the
Atlantic gales by a few battered trees. This is one of the many
Youth Hostels which provide overnight accommodation for
young people. Particulars from An Óige, 39 Mountjoy Square,
Dublin 1, and Youth Hostels Association, Bryson House, 28
Bedford Street, Belfast 2.*

Then screw your courage to the sticking point! It takes grit and determination to last the 15 mile canoe race on the River Shannon. These competitors are wielding their double-bladed paddles with a will during the Festival at Carrick-on-Shannon in 1971.
The Irish Canoe Union; the Central Student Union, Vocational School, Great Denmark Street, Dublin 1; the Association for Adventure Sports can give information on the subject.

forestry is "British Woodland Trees" by H. L. Edlin, published by Batsford and lavishly illustrated. Nature students should resist the temptation to collect birds' eggs or rare wild plants as this will lead to their decrease or extinction. This applies to Nature reserves especially—these are areas such as the native Sessile Oak reserves situated in Glengariff, Glendalough, Glen of the Downs, Derryclare (Co. Galway), Pontoon (Co. Mayo), Uragh Wood (Kenmare) and Killeary (Lough Gill)—where there is an unchanged vegetation reaching back to the primeval woods of Ireland.

A good general guide is the "Shell Country Book" by G. Grigson, Phoenix House Ltd. which, although intended for

England, contains much of interest for us in Ireland. It tells of wildlife in fields, hedgerows, woods and rivers, folklore and archaeology and is illustrated.

The Irish Biological Records Centre, which has offices with An Foras Forbartha, compiles records of wild animals and shows the location of species in Ireland on a series of maps. Animals included are Deer, Squirrel, Badger, Stoat, Fox and Hedgehog. "Trees for Ireland" publish booklets on trees and forestry.

The Association for Adventure Sports, Honorary Secretary 1971 at 99 Seapoint Avenue, Blackrock, Co. Dublin, gives instructions in these sports for the benefit of young learners. They include courses in canoeing, mountain climbing, diving and surfing. These pursuits are also catered for by their own clubs. The Surf Club has branches in Counties Wicklow, Antrim, Waterford and Limerick. Water Skiing Clubs with arrangements for speed boat hire are in many places around the coast and beside inland lakes. General information on surfing is available from "The Surf Club of Ireland", Mount Herbert, Bray, Co. Wicklow, and on Water Skiing there is a Bord Failte leaflet.

Surfing at Garrettstown, Co. Cork. Ireland has first class surf where the great Atlantic swells pound the beaches with waves as good as any in Australia. The Surf Club at Mount Herbert, Bray, supplies information.

Cruising on navigable rivers and lakes has become popular in recent times and cruising boats and barges can be hired on the Shannon, Lough Erne, Rivers Barrow, Suir and other places. The Shannon and its lakes have been developed for the cruising trade with marinas for mooring, fuelling and shopping for provisions. On dry land there is horse riding and pony trekking, catered for in many parts of the country with horses for hire and riding instruction. Horse-drawn caravans for touring and parked caravans can be rented at many centres.

Leaflets may be obtained from Bord Failte and Tourist Information Offices and from Northern Ireland Tourist Board, High St., Belfast.

To return to the water—skin diving and underwater swimming are popular sports in the clear seas of our North-west, West and South-west coasts, now organised by the Underwater Council, 22 Lakelands Close, Upper Kilmacud Road, Stillorgan, Co. Dublin, which will supply information on local facilities. Two major centres for Sailing are Dublin Bay and Cork Harbour, but there are dozens of other areas around our 2,000 miles of coastline.

Top left:
On the north coast near Coleraine is Portstewart with a fine strand flanked by black cliffs of Basalt, a rock peculiar to this part of Co. Derry and occurring over nearly the whole of Co. Antrim. Portstewart is a well developed seaside resort popular for bathing, boating, surfing and other water sports. All these activities hold peril for the non-swimmer and everyone should learn how to swim before venturing into the sea, rivers or lakes. The Water Safety Council and the Irish Amateur Swimming Association, Belfast, Dublin, Cork and Galway hold classes in many centres.

Bottom left:
Cruising on our "Inland Waterways"—the Shannon, the Erne, the Barrow and large lakes and the canals—is becoming a popular form of unusual holiday with opportunity for the close observation of wild life on the water and along the shore. The Shannon has marinas for re-fueling and provisioning and it and the Erne have been charted and furnished with marker buoys to indicate safe passages. Particulars of cruiser hiring may be obtained from Regional Tourist Offices and from hiring centres at Castle Archdale and Carrybridge on Lough Erne in Co. Fermanagh.

117

Our coast with its inlets and bays is ideal for sailing and most seaside towns have their yachting and dinghy clubs, such as Skerries, Malahide, Howth, Dun Laoghaire, Bray, Arklow, Wexford, Waterford, Youghal, Ballycotton, Cork, Kinsale, Baltimore, Dingle, Tralee, Rosses Point, Mullaghmore, Killybegs and inland on the Shannon Lakes and Lough Gill. There are twenty in Northern Ireland from Lough Swilly to Belfast Lough and County Down and one at Enniskillen on Lough Erne.
Some places have marinas with mooring and supply facilities and most provide yachts and dinghies on hire. There is sailing tuition at Dun Laoghaire, Malahide, Kinsale, Baltimore and other centres.

Kinsale has a yacht marina with mooring for eighteen boats and also gives week-long courses in the theory and practice of sailing. Information can be obtained from the Irish Yachting Association, 19A Tritonville Road, Dublin 4.

Quieter country entertainment may be found in visiting fine gardens and interesting and historic houses. Some belong to the State and others are privately owned and most of them charge a small fee. "The Historic Irish Tourist Houses and Gardens Association" lists thirty places open to the public in the Republic and nine in Northern Ireland. Important ones are Castletown

House, Celbridge; Howth Demesne; Tully, Kildare; Castlecoole and Florence Court, Enniskillen; Mount Usher, Co. Wicklow; Birr Castle; Westport House; Lissadell House, Castleward, Mount Stewart and Rowallane, Co. Down; and Bunratty Castle. There are also State properties which include Johnstown Castle, Co. Wexford; Muckross, Killarney; Avondale House and Forest, Co. Wicklow; and Forest Parks at Portglenone, Co. Antrim; Tollymore, Co. Down; Gortin Glen, Co. Tyrone; John F. Kennedy Park, Co. Wexford; Gougane Barra, Co. Cork; Dun a Ri, Kingscourt, Co. Cavan; Lough Key, Boyle.

It is worth knowing something about the ancient monuments which are so numerous in Ireland. Earthworks commonly referred to as "Raths", "Danish Forts" or "Fairy Rings" are to be found everywhere, there are about 30,000 of them. These were originally circular ramparts and ditches topped with timber palisades and were used to pen cattle and other farm animals at

Boating off the sandy shore of Cruit Island in West Donegal. The thousands of miles of coastline abounds in sheltered bays and inlets, perfect for fishing, for bird watching or for idle rowing.

119

Powerscourt, Enniskerry, is famous for its fine trees and for its beautiful gardens. The picture is of the sunken Japanese Garden with summer houses, little bridges over the stream and a coral rock grotto. The ironwork gates are notable.
The Dargle Waterfall, 400 feet high, is in the Deerpark, probably the first established in Ireland by the Normans, reached by a winding avenue which skirts the river for several miles.

Top left:
Pony trekking is catered for in many parts of the country and ponies may be hired and riding lessons arranged. The picture shows two riders in the Nier Valley, Comeragh Mountain, Co. Waterford. Regional Tourist offices have addresses.

Bottom left:
Gypsy Caravans can be hired in many centres. They are well equipped and amateurs are given instruction in the care of the horse, harnessing and driving. Centres for over-night stops are arranged along the routes. Regional Tourist Offices have addresses.

Top right:

Mount Usher at Ashford, Co. Wicklow, is one of the famous gardens of the world. Sixteen acres in extent it lies along the Vartry River which cascades over little waterfalls, its banks planted with many moisture loving flowers and trees. There are unusual species of trees and shrubs, Magnolias, Montezumae Pines, Camellias, Nothfagus, Eucalypts and the "Pocket Handkerchief Tree" Davidia, called after a French Jesuit Pere David, who discovered it in China. There is a Banana Plant which gets fruits but never ripens them.

Bottom right:

Slieve Donard was described by a Norman historian as "a very high mountain towering over the sea which flows between Britain and Ireland and named after St. Dominic who built a noble monastery at its foot".

The town of Newcastle is beside Tollymore Forest Park which stretches along the Shimna River into the hills. Here there are camping sites, marked trails and picnic places.

Passing through the Old Weir Bridge in the Lakes of Killarney, a thrilling moment in a boating trip. A ride in a jaunting car is another tourist attraction and the drivers are the best storytellers on earth with a legend about every landmark along their road by lake and dell.

night safe from wolves or marauders. In districts where stones were plentiful walls were built. These structures date from 600 A.D. to 1,000 A.D. Much older are the tombs, cairns, dolmens and stone circles such as the "passage" graves of the Boyne Valley at New Grange, Dowth and Knowth and at Loughcrew near Oldcastle—they belong to the Neolithic period, 3,000 B.C. The Stone Circle near Rosscarbery is from about 2,000 B.C. The

Left:
This beautiful old church at Kilfenora, Co. Clare, has been in use since early Christian times and is one of the many ancient churches to be seen all over Ireland. Some are a part of monasteries and such foundations often include a character- istic Irish building, the Round Tower, which were built by the monks as refuges during Danish hit and run raids. Bord Failte have issued an illustrated brochure on Ancient Monuments.

Gallarus Oratory, a few miles from Dingle in Co. Kerry, is one of the best preserved early Christian church buildings in Ireland. Built of unmortared stone it is still watertight after more than a thousand years. Near it is the Saint's Road, an ancient track said to have been made by St. Brendan to the summit of Brandon Mountain. Two miles away is Kilmal- kedar where there is a 12th century Hiberno-Ramanesque church, alphabet stone, ogham stone and small oratories.

early Christian period saw the building of monastic settlements of Glendalough and Clonmacnois and later those of Ardmore, Innisfallen, Freshford and Clonfert and many others. After the coming of the Normans in 1169 fortified castles were built—notable ones

Top right:
Gortin Glen Forest Park is in the Sperrin Mountains 5 miles north of Omagh in Co. Tyrone. It covers nearly 1,999 acres and has been developed as a recreation forest with trails for walking and pony trekking, sites for camping and a youth hostel. There is interesting wild life including a small herd of Japanese Sika deer, red squirrels and badgers.

Bottom right:
In Gortin Glen Forest Park near Omagh picnic sites are provided, complete with tables and benches. Picnic stoves are permitted, but not fires. There is also a stone built barbecue pit and log shelter.

This ancient grave slab, reputedly 1000 years old, is on Innismurray about 5 miles off the Sligo coast and reached by boat across the treacherous Innismurray Sound. A little monastery was formerly here but was destroyed by the Danes in A.D. 804 and only ruins remain.

126

are at Trim, the largest castle in Ireland built by de Lacey in 1205, Limerick, Adare, Carlow, Ferns and Roscommon. The castles at Bunratty, Carrick-on-Suir, Blarney and Ross near Killarney date from the 15th century. The arrival of continental Orders of monks—Benedictines, Franciscans, Cistercians and Augustinians—saw the building of great Gothic monasteries at Adare, Jerpoint, Nenagh, Dunbrody, Tintern, Graiguenamanagh, Boyle, Holy Cross and many other places.

There are booklets on Glendalough by M. V. Ronan, Adare by Wyndham Quin, Clonmacnois by B. Molloy and many leaflets published by the Regional Tourist Offices.

Booklets on country pursuits in the "I Spy" series which are of interest are: *At the Seaside, On the Farm, In the Country, Butterflies and Moths, Birds, In the Hedgerow.*

Staigue Fort, about 1½ miles up the hills above Castlecove on the Kenmare River, is one of the finest Prehistoric monuments in the country. The 18 feet high circular wall, with flights of steps on it, forms a ring almost ninety feet across and there are chambers within the thick walls. It is said to have been built in the late Bronze Age, about 500 B C.

Chapter VI

SPORTING ACTIVITIES

*Hunting, Shooting and Fishing with an outline of rules,
restrictions, seasons and customs.*

THERE are about twentyfive "Hunts" in the country which welcome visitors. These are located in Leinster, Munster, and in counties Galway and Mayo in Connacht, and a leaflet may be obtained from Bord Failte or the Regional Tourist Information Offices which gives the addresses of local secretaries who should be consulted before joining a meet. In general, hunting takes place only during the winter, from late October to early March, usually twice weekly, on Wednesdays and Saturdays. "Cap" fees are from £2 to £5 a day and horses may be hired at a cost of £8 to £12. In Northern Ireland consult the Tourish Board.

Shooting rights are privately owned and permission is necessary from farmers and other land owners before entering on land. In addition, the Land Commission and the Forest and Wildlife Service make annual lettings or give five year leases of the shooting rights of thousands of acres of estate, mountain and forest lands—particulars should be sought from the Department of Lands, Dublin. The Ministry for Agriculture in Belfast make similar lettings. In many parts shooting has been organised by local "gun clubs" and a list of the secretaries may be had from Tourist Information Offices. These gun clubs control the shooting over large areas and during the season some of them will provide guides and dogs to visitors at a charge of up to £10 per gun per day. The shooting is mainly "walk-up" rough shooting for snipe,

Up and over and mind your eyes on the thorns! Hunting is for the practised rider with a good horse and the nerve to face "hard leps" over banks and stone walls. Horses may be hired at centres in all hunting districts and Regional Tourist Offices will supply addresses. Costs £8 to £12 a day for horse and £2 to £5 cap fee to the Hunt.

woodcock, pheasant, pigeon and water birds including teal, mallard, wigeon and geese.

"Open Seasons" in 1971 were: Wild Duck, Wild Geese (all species except Brent, Barnacle and Greylag Geese), Plover (except Green Plover), Snipe and Woodcock—1st September to 31st January.

Grouse, Counties Cork, Kerry and Mayo—12th August to 30th September.

All other areas—1st September to 30th September.

Cock Pheasant—1st November to 31st January.

Partridge—1st November to 15 November.

A Firearms Certificate is necessary and should be obtained from the Department of Justice. The fee is £3.25 for a shot gun and £1.50 for a rifle. Particulars may be obtained from the local Garda Siochana station.

Deer Stalking is provided on some estates at a fee of up to £5 a day with an extra charge for all deer shot of up to £16 each.

Irish State Forests contain many species of game birds and deer and their management strives to provide food by leaving wide

Poised ready to spring forward, this gun dog awaits the order to retrieve the shot bird from a lake in Co. Wicklow.

131

The rapid zig-zag flight of a Snipe is a test for the quickest marksman. It lives in wet fields and swampy places where it feeds on worms, insects and small snails. During the breeding season snipe make a peculiar "drumming" sound by flying to a height and diving with its tail feathers held rigid so that they vibrate in the rush through the air.

Top left:
A happy party display their "bag" after a day with their dogs and guns.
There is good rough shooting nearly everywhere and a day's sport can be fixed with local landowners or a district gun club. The Department of Lands have a leaflet on shooting which gives dates of "close" seasons, what may and may not be shot and a list of the sanctuaries where all shooting is prohibited.
Guns are dangerous weapons! Always unload when climbing over a gate or fence and entering a house, never trail a loaded gun through a hedge and never let children touch it.

Bottom left:
The Grey Crow, Hooded Crow or Scald Crow as it is variously called is a solitary bird which builds its nest in woods and in bushes along cliffs remote from any of its kind. It is a much hated and constantly persecuted bird by farmers and sportsmen as it destroys eggs and young game birds and chickens and will peck out the eyes of newly born lambs. As it flies it utters a loud hoarse and raucous "caw".

Sika Deer, from Japan, were first brought to Powerscourt, Enniskerry, about 100 years ago and from there were distributed to many counties. There are herds in many forests in Counties Wicklow, Kerry, Limerick, Fermanagh, Tyrone and Down. The picture is of a female, a "Hind", in Killarney—worried by a swarm of flies around her head. The Sika is small, about 3 feet to the shoulders, and of a dun brown to sooty brown colour with a white tail. They give a sharp scream when alarmed and the rutting call of the stag is a long shrill whistle. The antlers have rarely more than 8 points which are rounded like those of the Red Deer and not flattened as in the Fallow Deer. They feed at night and in the early morning on grass, mosses and leaves of ivy, brambles and other shrubs.

grass rides and by the intermixture of berried trees and shrubs through the timber species. Young heather on which grouse feed is encouraged by the periodic burning of strips of heath land.

Certain game birds are protected in the Republic by Order for specified periods in addition to the normal off-seasons. The Game Birds Protection Order, 1971, prohibits the "killing or taking" in certain districts for twelve months of nearly all game birds including Pheasant, Partridge, Grouse, Snipe, Woodcock, Wild Duck and Wild Geese.

In Northern Ireland all birds are protected except predators and harmful species and, during the open season, game birds. Birds which are not protected include Cormorants, Mute Swan, Gull, Wood Pigeon, Hooded Crow, Rook, Jackdaw, Magpie, Jay, Starling, Bullfinch and House Sparrow. Special protection covers Swans, except Mute Swans, Whimbrel, Plover, Rock and Stock Dove, Redshank, Curlew and all species of Geese and Ducks and

"A central limestone plain traversed by deep, slow rivers and clear streams lush with buttercup and starwort, feeding great trout Loughs. Mountains rimming the coast, veined with tumbling streams."

That is Ireland as the angler sees it, in the words of a Bord Failte leaflet which gives information on Salmon, Trout, Coarse Fishing and Sea Angling, locations, seasons and fees payable to angling associations and for licences.

Here, pictured in a pool on the lower reach of the River Dun near Cushendun, Co. Antrim, an angler enjoys the oldest sport in the world. The lore of the fisherman is unending and useful books are "A Book on Angling" by Francis and a booklet "Fish and Fishing" in the "I Spy" series.

their eggs and nests during the close season from 1st February to 31st August. Barnacle, Brent and Canada Geese are specially protected at all times.

Fishing is free on many of the large lakes—Corrib, Mask, Carra, Conn, Arrow, Derg, Killarney, Erne, Neagh—and on some small lakes and rivers. The best salmon fisheries are preserved and are let by the day, week or month. Some are owned by hotels and are reserved for their guests and angling clubs control other waters. A rod licence is required for salmon and sea trout fishing and in

Beside the Mournes on Castlewellan Lake in the amphi-theatre of a Forest Park, a fisherman casts his line. For peace, for solitude in beautiful surroundings no sport equals this.
The methods employed are numerous and vary with the season, the weather, the waters fished and the fish sought and maybe with the whim of the fisher! There is bottom fishing with bait and float, mid-water fishing which is spinn-ing, trolling or live-baiting and top or surface fishing with live or artificial flies as bait, and variations of these. The names given to artificial flies made from feathers of all colours include—"The Blue Doctor", used on the Lee, "The Orange Antony" popular on the Blackwater, and "The Green Grouse" said to be good on the Bann!

One for the grill! Lough Oughter in Co. Cavan, like other clear limestone lakes of the Central Plain such as Sheelin, Derravaragh, Owel, Ennell, Carra and Arrow provides wet fly fishing for trout in March, April, early May and September and dry fly fishing during the May fly hatch, mid-May and early June, and on summer evenings. The average weight of Brown Trout is 2 lb. and may be as high as 4 lb.

Lough Oughter is the most southerly of a maze of lakes, islands and peninsulas which lie in the triangle between Cavan, Killeshandra and Belturbet along the course of Upper River Erne.

137

the Republic it costs £1 for seven days, £3 for the season in a single fishery district and £4 for a full season in all fishing districts. The Inland Fisheries Trust, a State agency working in co-operation with angling clubs, controls many lakes and rivers, on most of which its members may fish for brown trout. An annual fee of about 50p is charged. Other trout waters are controlled by angling associations with an annual subscription up to £2 per year.

In 1349 the Abbot of Mellifont, the Cistercian Abbey just north of the river, built a Salmon Weir at Oldbridge on the Boyne which is still there. Just below is the site of the Battle where in July 1690 the Williamite cavalry crossed in a decisive move towards victory in one of the world's momentous conflicts.

The Boyne provides Spring fishing for salmon in late March and early April.

For "Coarse" fish, i.e. Pike, Perch, Bream, Tench and Carp, the best fishing is in the Shannon, the Erne and the slow-running rivers, small lakes and canals of the Central Plain and in Roscommon, Sligo, east Galway, east Mayo, east Clare, Leitrim, Cavan, Monaghan, Westmeath, Longford, Offaly and parts of Louth. The Rivers Barrow and Blackwater are good. Roach and Dace are found only in the Blackwater in Munster. There is Shark Fishing at Kinsale and Achill.

The European Coarse Fishing Championship at Fermoy, Co.
Cork. From here, where the River Blackwater skirts the lime-
stone plains of North Cork, through Ballyduff, and Lismore
and down to Cappoquin, is the best salmon fishing on this
famous river. The Blackwater and its tributary the Bride
holds Salmon, Trout, Roach, Dace and Fluke. The season for
Game fishing is from 1st February to 30th September and all
year for Coarse fishing. Salmon of 35 lbs. have been caught
in the Lismore fishery.
For Coarse fishing we hear that the best bait is maggot
obtainable locally—but it must be ordered in advance.

No rod licence is required for brown trout.

The salmon season opens on a few rivers on January 1st—
Liffey and Garvogue. On most rivers it is 1st February, 26th
February on Slaney and 1st May on the Bangor Erris streams in
Mayo. It ends on 30th September except the Slaney, 31st August
and Boyne, 15th September. Some rivers provide salmon fishing
in Spring, in March and April; these include the Boyne, Nore,
Suir and Munster Blackwater. There is also summer fishing for
salmon on the smaller lakes and rivers of Kerry, Connemara and
Donegal.

There is free sea trout fishing in several lakes—Lough Currane, Waterville and Caragh Lake and in many coastal streams where sea trout are to be found after a flood. They can also be caught in salt water in a number of places and this fishing is mostly free but requires a salmon rod licence.

Excellent sea angling is found off the south and west coasts— light spinning for bass in estuaries and from boats and rock fishing for Pollack, Wrasse, Conger and Tope. Blue shark fishing is available at Dungarvan, Achill, Kinsale and Ballycotton where boats with experienced boatmen may be hired.

The best coarse fishing is in the Shannon, the Erne and the slow flowing rivers, small lakes and canals of the Central Plain in Sligo, Roscommon, East Galway, East Mayo, East Clare, Leitrim, Cavan, Monaghan, Westmeath, Longford, Offaly and parts of Louth. The Barrow and Munster Blackwater are both excellent. Coarse fishing includes Pike, Perch, Rudd, Bream, Tench, and, in the Blackwater, Roach and Dace.

No rod licence is required.

Information on fishing may be had from Bord Failte or from Regional Tourist Information Offices and Northern Ireland Tourist Board.

A good small book is "Fish and Fishing" published in the "I Spy" series by the Dickens Press. Bord Failte publish four booklets on fishing: Salmon, Brown Trout, Sea Fishing and Coarse Fishing.

Recently published by Warne is "The Observer's Book of Sea Fishes" by T. B. Bagenal.

Right:
Rock climbing is one of the most challenging of sports and the feeling of triumph of this white shirted climber, now half-way up the cliff face, when he reaches the top can be imagined. Safe climbing calls for a steady head and proper training and needs the right clothes, boots and equipment—novices who tackle it on their own are looking for trouble.

The Irish Mountaineering Club, P.O. Box 109, Dublin 1, may be consulted about training and guide books about the sport in Dublin, Wicklow, Galway, Donegal and Kerry and can give contacts for Antrim, Fermanagh and Down.

141

Orienteering is the art of finding the way over unknown ground with the aid of a map and compass. Competitions are cross-country runs of 3 to 7 miles through hilly, wooded country, checking at control points along the route. Courses are held by clubs in Dublin, Belfast and Cork: information from Hon. Sec., Irish Orienteering Association, Woodside, Sandyford, Co. Dublin.

142

Chapter VII

CONSERVATION

*The danger of destroying the countryside, its trees, hedges, streams
and lakes by ill-judged development, industrial and
agricultural pollution and careless waste disposal.*

IRELAND is changing from a largely rural and pastoral country
into an urban and industrial one and there is a danger that much
of its natural beauty will be lost as a result of thoughtless
development. Conservation, of which we heard so much in 1970,
does not mean keeping everything as it is. That would be stagna-
tion. Change is inevitable. Trees grow up and mature and should
be felled for the value of their timber before it deteriorates. Buildings become old and unsuited to modern needs and should be
pulled down and rebuilt. Factories must be built as they are
essential to manufacture our needs and to provide employment.
All these changes must be accepted; good conservation aims to
do these things in such a way that the country, the "environment"
as the conservationists say, in which we live should not be destroyed.

Sudden change is to be avoided if things which are worth keeping are to be saved. Maintenance and gradual change should be
the aim. A period of neglect is nearly always followed by a period
of drastic change with wholesale destruction. Trees are left standing far beyond their proper life-span until finally whole districts
are denuded of all trees because they have become unsafe or take
up too much room. This is all too often the fate of street and
roadside trees. A programme of removal and replacement would

143

aim at taking out occasional trees and replanting, so that the over-all appearance would remain unspoilt. Hedges, too, can suffer in this way. For years they are left untrimmed and then, when they have become a wilderness of trees, bushes and brambles, they are subjected to draconian treatment by mechanical hedge-trimmers which level them nearly to the ground or they are uprooted by bull-dozer. Annual trimming keeps hedges at a reasonable height and width and they fulfill their function of sheltering cattle and sheep against wind, keeping these animals within bounds and at the same time giving refuge and nesting places to small birds.

A clear sparkling fast flowing stream is one of the joys of the countryside! Many are spoilt by careless people dumping rubbish, or using them as sewers or by farmers allowing the drainage from silage to reach them—it is reckoned that the effluent from a silage clamp will cause as much pollution and kill as many fish in a river as the sewage from a city of 166,000 people for a week. Pollution of this nature causes the death of fish and other water creatures by using up the oxygen on which they depend.
The picture shows the Glendun River in the Glens of Antrim which is good for fishing.

This little family can be wiped out by oil spillage or other gross pollution of the water. Not only is there danger along the coast and in estuaries but also in lakes and rivers where waste oil emptied into garage drains may end up—and we use nearly 11 million gallons of lubricating oil each year.

*A Barn Owl taking a mouse to its young in a hollow tree
trunk. Very often this bird lives in belfries or church towers
and its appearance as it flits at dusk amongst the tombstones,
at times uttering a loud weird shriek, then a whistling cry
or a low snoring sound, must surely have given rise to many
ghost stories.*
*It is very scarce now and it seems that it has been poisoned
by eating mice themselves affected by feeding on grain treated
with poisonous seed dressing.*

146

In recent years the world has awakened to the dire effects of pollution of stream, lake and the sea by the discharge of waste from factories and from town sewage. Remedies include settling tanks to separate solids from industrial effluents and chemical treatment to remove toxic materials, and, for sewage, an aeration process to oxidise organic matter so that rivers are not robbed of the oxygen in the water which is vital to fish and other aquatic life.

This purification of effluents and, where possible, the "re-cycling" of waste matter to separate materials which can be used again, is, of course, a matter for local authorities and industrial organisations. The individual can reduce pollution, however, by taking care in the disposal of paper wrappings, bottles, tins and other containers which are so common. These ought not to be left scattered on road verges, forest paths or picnic places or on the

A Heron, or Crane as it is usually named, will be seen on most rivers, standing still on the look-out for fish or eels, or slowly flapping its way, with an occasional "Frank-Frank" call. As well as fish it will eat frogs, snails, worms and even rats and mice. The nests are usually in colonies, "Heronries", in the top-most branches of high trees.

147

The Bewick Swan winters in our coastal waters, arriving from Siberia and the far north in November and December and departing in March or April. It feeds on water plants and, during the Summer, on insects. The cry of the Bewick sounds like "tong" or "bong" quickly uttered.

seashore, nor ought they to be flung into rivers. Plastic bags and bottles are long lasting and besides being unsightly, there have been cases of cattle being choked by trying to eat plastic bags carelessly thrown over farm hedges.

The use of chemicals in the growing of many crops is now standard practice both as fertilisers to promote growth and as sprays to kill fungus and bacterial diseases and insect pests. The excessive and continuous effects of some of the substances used can have a deleterious effect on many forms of wildlife. Birds can be killed by eating poisoned insects, owls, kestrels and other birds of prey may suffer by feeding on smaller birds and mice suffering from poison, and fish in rivers and lakes can be destroyed by farm chemicals carried by streams. Another form of agricultural pollution comes from sheep dipping tanks and a further one is caused by the drainage from grass silage pits, cattle yards and piggeries finding its way into water courses. Farmers are urged to consult their agricultural advisers about these matters.

There is now a general awareness of the dangers of these threats to the countryside and more people than ever before are interested in nature conservation. The Planning Act exercises control on the siting of factories in order to reduce any ill-effects on the district. The concept of "multiple-use" of State forests has drawn attention to the need of making them attractive to visitors as well as to birds and animals by a mixture of species, especially broadleaved

A Magpie arriving home at her untidy nest. This large black and white bird does good by devouring slugs, worms, insects, rats and mice but meets with little approval from sportsmen as it feeds on the eggs and young of game birds. At one time plentiful, it is now rare in many parts of the country, probably the victim of poisons eaten by the creatures on which it feeds.

The Sandwich Tern, or Sea Swallow as it is sometimes called on account of its long tail feathers and speed in flight, gets its name from a sea-port in Kent where it was first seen. It is a migrant and comes to us about May and leaves in August— there are nesting colonies around the coast, the one in the picture is in Co. Wexford. Terns, like other sea birds, are killed by a scum of oil on the water.

species, through the masses of conifers. An increasing interest in wildfowl has shown that the drainage of swamps and marshes may destroy the wintering ground of thousands of migratory birds— for instance, one half of the world's population of White Fronted Geese winter on the Wexford North Slob which was threatened by a large scheme of drainage until a reservation was established there by the Department of Lands. Recently a 700 acre wild fowl refuge was provided around Kilcolman Castle near Doneraile— Co. Cork consisting of bog and marsh and has received recognition by the European Association for Free Nature Reserves.

Bottom right:
Twenty feet down in the clear waters of Bantry Bay the under-water photographer meets many strange and beautiful marine animals. Surely the lovliest is the Starfish gliding gracefully through the water in search of molluscs on which it feeds.

Jelly Fish are known as Sea Nettles because they are able to sting. The "umbrella" is composed of a transparent jelly with a fringe of delicate Cilia which wave as it travels through the water.

High in the swaying tree top these baby Herons manage to remain in their clumsy nest of sticks as they await the return of the mother bird with a frog or maybe a trout for dinner.

Top right:
The Merlin is a small Falcon found in bogs and mountains and in winter on the seashore where it preys on Snipe, Dunlins and other small birds. It is docile and may be trained to hunt and retrieve partridges and small game birds.

Bottom right:
Young as he is, this Merlin chick will not easily let "his bone go with any dog".

Every horse has a dash of Arab blood and thoroughbred race-horses are closely related to the pure Arabian strain which is "light in body, neck long and arched, eye full and soft, and leg delicate and slender, with a remarkably sweet temper". Let's hope this gay little chap grows up that way.

[OVERLEAF]

Who is the most surprised, the Fox, the Coot or the Swans? The Fox leaves his "earth", a deep burrow with several entrances, in the early morning to go ahunting and will gladly pounce on a rabbit or a lamb or will raid a hen roost. If nothing better offers he will make do with a few frogs or a rat or two.

Coots resemble Water Hens but, have a white patch on their heads. They live on lakes, ponds and rivers and feed on weeds, water insects and worms. The Swan on the right is a young bird, a Cygnet, sooty grey in colour before its first moult.

Chapter VIII

SAFETY IN THE COUNTRY

*A few tips for inexperienced adults and those in charge
of children visiting country places.*

COUNTRY pursuits present dangers to the inexperienced and nearly
all of them call for training if injury or even fatalities are to be
avoided. Perhaps the greatest perils lie in the water—every summer sees the deaths of young people who bathe in dangerous
places without an elementary knowledge of swimming. Others,
complete novices to the art of boating, calmly embark on lakes
or the sea and "hope for the best". Swimming lessons are given
in many schools and swimming clubs and tuition in boating and
sailing is provided in Malahide, Kinsale, Dun Laoighaire, and
other places. Ice, too, needs to be approached warily: a frozen
pond could be a death trap if the ice is not strong enough for
skating or sliding and local advice should always be obtained.

For horse riding there are dozens of schools all over the
country—a leaflet is available from the Regional Tourist Offices.

Mountaineering, especially rock climbing, should not be en-
tered on without proper instruction and proper equipment. Even
a walk across an open hillside or bog can be dangerous for anyone
who does not know the way and especially for those without
proper clothes and footwear—a light city suit and flimsy shoes
are quite wrong on a mountain. A small pocket compass is useful
too in case fog or a mountain mist should come down.

The risk of careless handling of firearms should need no stress-
ing but many accidents occur from neglect of a few rules: unload
before climbing over a gate or fence, or when entering a house;

155

never pull a loaded gun through a hedge and, in the house, keep guns and ammunition out of the reach of children.

With ordinary common-sense, farms can be perfectly safe places and children may join in many tasks without likelihood of injury.

This Shorthorn may not be dangerous; who likes being disturbed at breakfast? It is wise for strangers to steer clear of all cattle, especially if they have a dog along.

Tiny lambs are about the only animals on a farm which are safe for children to cuddle, and they soon grow too big.

They should not be carried as passengers on tractors or other machines and it is well to keep them at a distance when mowing machines, balers or combine harvesters are operating. It goes without saying that amateur drivers should not be allowed on tractors; the ability to drive a car is not sufficient for the job.

Farm animals generally are harmless but it is as well for outsiders to keep away from cattle as they often resent strangers and may stampede especially if there is a strange dog. Most people will take care to keep a safe distance from a bull but not everyone realizes that a ram may be a menace too. Animals with young are often a bit edgy, and a sow or a cow which are normally harmless can become wicked at these times.

Children should beware of pits of liquid manure, slurry pits the farmers call them, as the surface can look deceptively solid and invite walking.

A few other country things need watching. Drinking water should be taken only from wells, pumps and springs used by local people—rivers and streams are not safe, even mountain streams

may be contaminated. Wild fruits and berries should not be eaten as many are poisonous. Caution is needed with mushrooms and only the ordinary sort picked fresh in a pasture field is recommended although enthusiasts claim that many toadstools are edible too. Wild water cress may not be safe. The water in which it grows may be impure or it may be an unwholesome plant resembling ordinary water cress.

To enjoy the countryside in safety:

KEEP on the right side of the farmers !

KEEP away from farm animals.

KEEP off tractors and agricultural machines.

KEEP closed gates that way.

KEEP to regular paths as far as possible.

KEEP away from rock and cliff climbing unless trained.

KEEP out of lakes, rivers and the sea if unable to swim.

KEEP with companions on country rambles - the solitary walker can get into difficulties.

KEEP from eating strange fruits and berries and drinking water of unknown source.

KEEP an eye on children.

Top left:
Beware of the Bull! Nobody needs a second warning if one of these big fellows is loose.

Bottom left:
This shaggy buck goat with his supercilious expression might well have a go at a stranger and it is well to steer clear of him—a butt from a goat travelling at speed can hurt.

162

The aims of the worldwide Youth Hostels Associations are the same as those of An Oige, "to help all, but especially young people, to a love and appreciation of the countryside particularly by providing simple hostel accommodation for them on their travels. Membership is open to all who love to walk and cycle—there is no age limit".

Members of An Oige and the Northern Ireland Youth Hostels Association are entitled to use about 60 hostels all over Ireland in old castles and cottages, shooting lodges and disused coastguard stations, former schools and military barracks.

Left:

Exploring caves and underground passages is the challenging sport of Speleologists. It needs training and equipment and should be done only in organised groups. Solitary explorers and inexperienced amateurs are in danger of getting lost.

There are clubs in Belfast, Cork, Dublin and Kilkenny. The Hon. Sec. of the Speleological Association is c/o Geography Department, Trinity College, Dublin 2.

Illustrated opposite is the Market Cross Stalagmite, Dunmore Cave, Co. Kilkenny.

Every gardener knows that as soon as he turns up the soil with spade or fork a Robin is bound to arrive to pounce on any worm or grub revealed by the digging. It is our most familiar bird, resident the whole year although there are migrants too, and in cold weather very ready to come near to houses for food and shelter.

ILLUSTRATIONS

The author is appreciative of the kindness of Departments of State, Tourist Boards and other institutions, newspapers, professional and private photographers who supplied the photographs which are such an important feature of this book.

INTRODUCTION

CHAPTER I—WHO OWNS THE COUNTRY?

CHAPTER II—COUNTRY WORK

165

CHAPTER III—THE FACE OF IRELAND

Views—Republic of Ireland — Bord Failte
Views—Northern Ireland — Northern Ireland Tourist Board
Tuskar Rock Lighthouse/Bog Pool, Co. Mayo — Dr. David Cabot, An Foras Forbartha
Lough Gill, Church Island and Lake — Department of Lands
E.S.B. Pylons — Irish Farmers' Journal
Dargle Glen — Dermot Barry, Irish Times
Tynagh Mine — Sam Edgar Public Relations

CHAPTER IV—WILD LIFE IN WOODS, FIELDS, MOUNTAINS, BOGS, SEASHORE, LAKES AND STREAMS

Blackbird/Blue Titmouse/Skylark/ Pied Wagtail/Sparrowhawk/Long-eared Owl/House Sparrow/ Chaffinch/Seals — R. T. Mills, Cork
Swans at Oakpark, Carlow — Des McDonough, Carlow
Wild Duck's Nest/Whooper Swan/ Gannets on Little Skellig (lower)/ Pigeons/Red Deer/Toad/Goats on Dalkey Island/Otter/Wild Rabbit — Irish Times
Oyster Catchers — Pat Langan, Irish Times
Pair of Mallard Ducks — Bord Failte
Gannets on Little Skellig (upper)/ Common Terns/Fallow Deer/ Lizard/Pipewort — Dr. David Cabot, An Foras Forbartha
Dandelion — Tom Kennedy, Stream & Field
Wild Flowers on Slea Head — Stream & Field

CHAPTER V—COUNTRY PURSUITS

Views—Northern Ireland — Northern Ireland Tourist Board